D0862543

The Preacher and the Politician

THE PREACHER AND THE POLITICIAN

Jeremiah Wright, Barack Obama, and Race in America

CLARENCE E. WALKER AND
GREGORY D. SMITHERS

UNIVERSITY OF VIRGINIA PRESS
CHARLOTTESVILLE AND LONDON

University of Virginia Press

Printed in the United States of America on acid-free paper

First published 2009
First paperback edition published 2012
ISBN 978-0-8139-3247-7 (paper)

1 3 5 7 9 8 6 4 2

The Library of Congress has cataloged the hardcover edition as follows:

LIBRARY OF CONGRESS CATALOGING-IN-PUBLICATION DATA

Walker, Clarence Earl.
The preacher and the politician : Jeremiah Wright, Barack Obama, and race in America / Clarence E. Walker and Gregory D. Smithers.
p. cm.
Includes bibliographical references and index.
ISBN 978-0-8139-2886-9 (cloth : acid-free paper)
1. Obama, Barack. 2. Wright, Jeremiah A., Jr. 3. United States—Race relations—Political aspects. 4. United States—Race relations—Religious aspects. 5. Post-racialism—United States. 6. Presidents—United States—Biography. 7. African American clergy—Biography. 8. African American churches. 9. Protestantism—Political aspects—United States. 10. Chicago (Ill.)—Politics and government—1951– I. Smithers, Gregory D., 1974– II. Title.
E908.3.W35 2009
973.932092—dc22 2009014341

Contents

The Preacher and the Politician

"They Didn't Give Us Our Mule and Our Acre"

Introduction

"They didn't give us our mule and our acre, but things are better."[1] With these words, Miss Harris, a sixty-seven-year-old veteran of the civil rights movement, celebrated Barack Obama's stunning victory over his Republican Party rival, John McCain, in the 2008 presidential election. Obama became the forty-fourth president of the United States and the first president to self-identify as "black." Obama's victory was as stunning for its comprehensiveness as it was for the way his candidacy focused American attention on the enduring legacy of race in the United States.[2] For African Americans, Harris's celebratory remarks typify the lived history of race in America: while lamenting the unfulfilled dreams of the past—the promise of "forty acres and a mule" after the Civil War—she also looks optimistically to an Obama presidency as proof that black Americans will finally enjoy genuine equality in America, an equality that can come only with the sharing of political power.

Obama's victory was a truly momentous moment in American history. But amid the jubilation of millions of Americans—black, white, Asian, and Hispanic—after Obama's historic triumph, the fact remains that on November 4, 2008, voters in many states also cast ballots on initiatives relating to abortion, affirmative action, and gay marriage, initiatives that underlined the hotly contested—and interrelated—issues of race, gender, and sexuality in modern America. In Colorado and Nebraska, for instance, voters rejected race- and gender-based affirmative action schemes (in Arizona, Missouri, Nebraska, and Oklahoma, insufficient signatures were collected to place similar initiatives on the November 4 ballot).[3] In Florida, Arizona, and California, voters rejected ballot options to legalize gay marriage, while in Arkansas, voters overwhelmingly supported a ballot measure that prevented unmarried heterosexual and gay couples from adopting children. Race, gender, and sexuality, so often the source of fissure in American society and politics, remain—in spite of Obama's victory and the hope that he inspires for a more tolerant future—contentious issues that reflect how America's past continues to shape its present.[4]

Obama's candidacy, and his stunning electoral victory, highlighted the historical contradictions that have made the United States what it has been and that continue to shape what it is becoming. The son of a white mother from Kansas and a Kenyan father, Obama uses stirring oratory to connect with millions of Americans who identify with his mixed-race heritage. Others, desperate to rekindle faith in the democratic ideals that have attracted millions of immigrants to American shores, hang on Obama's every word, hoping to hear reassurance that the "American dream" of upward socioeconomic mobility is still possible. Thus, on November 4, 2008, millions of Americans cast their ballots for a leader they hope will reinvigorate the United States with a sense of hope and optimism. Obama has revived these sentiments in a world that so often appears divided by race, wealth, and religion. As one euphoric Chicagoan put it, Obama can help "bridge the racial divide in Chicago. . . . Black people and white people now have a common aspirational [*sic*] figure and icon in Obama, someone who can lead both races."[5]

While Obama embodies the hope of a better, fairer, and more

egalitarian America to some Americans, others view him as an inexperienced, radical, unpatriotic, and foreign figure. Those who express these views are situated on the far right of American politics (though they often describe themselves as defenders of "traditional" American values). The Web site Conservapedia, for example, states that Obama was "allegedly born in Hawaii," that his "background and education are Muslim," and that, between 1988 and 2008, he was a member of Reverend Jeremiah Wright's Trinity United Church of Christ in Chicago, a church that "was the first in America to ordain gays, women and blacks as ministers."[6] Obama has also been accused of being a "secret Muslim," of having connections with radical institutions, and of being a Marxist and an elitist, all of which led critics to charge that he was a subversive threat to "conservative" American values, a threat that inspired more than five hundred death threats during his 2008 campaign for the White House.[7]

Modern Americans experience race and racism in various ways. While the crude pseudoscientific racism of antebellum America, the Jim Crow South, and the Massive Resistance campaigns opposing court-ordered integration in the 1950s and 1960s has become attenuated, race and racism remain lived realities that structure many aspects of American life.[8] Indeed, to truly understand American history requires the uncomfortable realization that race has been—and continues to be—the central fissure in American society. Crude forms of racism—repugnant to most in modern America—continue to exist among marginalized members of American society. One white supremacist Web site offers an example of an extreme form of contemporary racism, labeling Obama a "subhuman-black-supremeist-shitskin-beast" who will destroy the "white race."[9] Other expressions of racial hatred are shocking for the context in which they are expressed. In Florida, for instance, the Jackson County School Board endured national media scrutiny after a seventh-grade teacher presented students with these words: "CHANGE—Come Help a Nigger Get Elected."[10] And in small-town Ohio,

Halloween celebrations for one homeowner involved hanging a white-sheeted effigy of Obama from a tree.[11]

To most Americans, such racism is anachronistic in an age when multiculturalism, "color blindness," and racial "tolerance" are espoused as core American values. However, it is important to note that these apparently anachronistic racial views were expressed, and reported on, in a variety of media outlets. Given the variety of media sources cited in this book—from the right-wing blogs and the sensationalist reporting of the Fox News Channel to newspapers such as the *New York Times*—the question arises: what constitutes "mainstream" media and public opinion? Millions of Americans would identify Fox's *O'Reilly Factor* as "mainstream" media reporting. According to Nielsen television rankings, the *O'Reilly Factor* regularly outperforms other cable news channels, with between 2.5 million and 4 million viewers on any given day.[12] Recent research has also found that young, college-educated Americans—the millions who voted for Obama in November 2008—get their news from Comedy Central's *Daily Show.*[13] These viewing habits have the potential to redefine our understanding of "mainstream" news media; indeed, they may result in competing definitions. One of the traditional standard-bearers of "mainstream" news coverage, the PBS *NewsHour,* lags behind both the *Daily Show* and the *O'Reilly Factor,* with approximately 1 percent of the nation's viewers tuning in to its nightly broadcast. While the *NewsHour* is not a cable news broadcast, academics and middle-class professionals generally perceive PBS reporting—with its experts, academics, and in-depth reporting—as closer to the model of "mainstream" thinking.[14] Obviously, many different conclusions can be drawn from ratings and statistics; what is clear, however, is that for millions of Americans, the views expressed on Comedy Central and the Fox News Channel are not only becoming mainstream, they have become the preferred norm. To simply dismiss these views as marginal is to do an injustice to the cross-section of views that influence the decision making of millions of Americans.

The Democratic Party's southern wing, for example, attempts to draw its support from this cross-section of public opinion. The southern Democratic Party claims that it embraces a "New Southern Strategy," a political strategy that emphasizes moving the South beyond its "history of racial discord" by focusing on the economic issues that concern "prosperous suburb-dwellers."[15] Historians of the American South will no doubt recognize these themes. In the 1890s, the "Promise of the New South" rested on economic development. The leaders of the "New South" framed their political rhetoric of economic progress in ways that also silenced black voices.[16] They did this by instituting a slew of Jim Crow laws that disenfranchised and segregated African American people. Thus, race was not a "problem" in the "New South" because the "Negro problem," as it was called, had been legislated to the margins of southern society.[17]

While the proponents of the "New Southern Strategy" do not express any plan for reinstituting legal segregation, their ranks are filled with people who proclaim to be "pro-gun," "pro-life," and "anti-illegal immigration," and who deal with race by pretending it does not exist or by, in the language of the "New Southern Strategy," "moving beyond racial discord."[18] This strategy aims to win back to the Democratic Party those poorer and working-class white voters who began voting for the Republican Party during Ronald Reagan's two terms as president. However, the "New Southern Strategy" is fraught with electoral peril because race continues to shape life in the South. For example, in the 2006 Senate race in Tennessee, Harold Ford Jr., an African American who had served five terms as a congressman, lost to his Republican rival, Bob Corker, after a television advertisement depicted an attractive blond woman asking Ford to "call me."[19] In 2008, Obama's campaign also had to maneuver around the sexually charged history of race, race mixing, and radicalism. This was a delicate balancing act for the Obama campaign team, as the controversy surrounding his twenty-year relationship with Reverend Wright, combined with suspicions raised by his Muslim name, gave new life to old fears about the political objectives of a mixed-race political figure. Was Obama, as some of his critics argued, a white-hating black nationalist? Was he really a Muslim? Was he really "not one of us"? Did he fail, as one of his opponents put it, "to see America like you and I see America"?[20] In his memoir *Dreams from My Father,* Obama hinted at the difficulties to which such labels give rise when he quoted 1 Chronicles 29:15: "For we are strangers before them, and sojourners, as were all our fathers."[21] Questions of race and "otherness" dogged the first black presidential candidate throughout 2008. One southerner, for example, told a *Newsweek* reporter, "They say that they caught him [Obama] trying to sneak Iraqi soldiers into the United States." Thus, the "New Southern Strategy" appears to be operating in a South where many old prejudices still resonate for some.

During the 2008 presidential campaign, a number of the racial statements that scholars term "coded messages"—phrases such as "states' rights," "welfare queens," and affirmative action—became more overtly racial. Obama, for example, endured endless ridicule about his middle name—Hussein—in addition to erroneous taunts that "he [was] a Muslim." In addition, opponents crudely mocked Obama with placards that read "Obama Bin Lyin," and insinuated that he, because of his association with Jeremiah Wright, was racist toward whites. Conservative media personalities derided Obama's *Dreams from My Father,* with Ann Coulter calling it a "dimestore *Mein Kampf.*" Coulter and other extreme right-wing commentators fueled fears about Obama's foreignness by insinuating that he subscribed to Marxist and Black Power doctrines. Republican vice-presidential nominee Sarah Palin attempted to reinforce these negative perceptions of Obama when she asserted that he had spent his adult life "palling around with terrorists."[22] Subtle forms of racialism were also expressed during the 2008 presidential campaign, including repeated and thinly veiled claims that Obama is a cunning, shiftless mixed-race politician, sentiments that were embodied in statements such as "we don't really know him," "he lacks experience," and "he has a split personality."[23] These forms of racialism are so deeply embedded in American history and culture that most Americans do not recognize that the rearticulation of these old racial stereotypes constitutes a highly racialized worldview from the American past that continues to inform the present. While the United States has moved beyond the racism of the 1860s and, for that matter, the 1960s, millions of Americans continue to live with the effects of race, something that is rarely discussed in an open and frank manner in American society. Indeed, to discuss the significance of race in American society would seem to call into question, in the minds of a growing number of Americans, the increasingly common, if misleading, assumption that the United States has entered a "postracial" age.

In twenty-first-century America, racial prejudice—whether it is overt or implicit—is not meant to exist. According to a growing cadre of journalists and scholars who write about the United States as a "postracial" society, and Obama as the epitome of a "postracial" political candidate, nineteenth and twentieth-century racism are anachronistic in modern America.[24] The conceptualization of the United States as "postracial" emphasizes America's multiracial diversity. "Postrace" scholars often use jargonistic language, emphasizing what they describe as "deconstructive approaches to identities, . . . theories of performativity, passing, and new ethnicities," to define an essentially "color-blind" society in which "old essentialist views of biological races" are consigned to a dark and forgotten chapter in American history.[25] A number of conservative commentators have pounced on "color-blind" rhetoric to challenge affirmative action programs. For example, Fox News Channel's Bill O'Reilly claims that affirmative action can only be "fair to everybody on an equal basis" if it is based on income level, not race, because "I don't believe color is the American way."[26]

The chapters that follow place Barack Obama, his relationship with Reverend Jeremiah Wright and the black church, and Obama's own mixed-race heritage and politics into historical perspective. As we demonstrate, "postracial" and "color-blind" rhetoric serves only to silence substantive historical discussions of race and racism in America's history, society, and contemporary politics.[27] Placed in historical context, "postracial" theories do not enable racialized peoples to transcend race; on the contrary, they involve the deployment of new terminology that reinscribes old racial binaries of white and nonwhite. The increasingly popular "postracial" theories in effect proclaim whiteness as normative. This, in large part, explains the media firestorm and public outrage that followed Reverend Wright's critique of racism in American society. How, after all, can you critique something that is no longer supposed to exist in American society? That "postracialism" reinscribes whiteness as normative also explains why supporters of "postracial" ideals have a difficult time acknowledging that Obama is *black*, an identity that he himself has publicly embraced. To deny Obama the right to define his own racial subjectivity is to brandish the illiberal club of racial essentialism that has for four hundred years characterized white racism in North America and attempted to marginalize black people and "blackness" from all walks of American life. All of this suggests that twenty-first-century Americans remain uncomfortable with the modern implications of their racial history. As the British journalist Andrew Rawnsley observed in August 2008, "It seems a paradox, but perhaps it is not, that race is the hardest thing for America to talk about during its first election in which a black man is a serious contender for the presidency."[28]

Rawnsley's observation is borne out by the Obama literature that has proliferated in bookstores across the United States, and throughout the world, over the past two years. From popular political magazines—such as *Time*, the *New Republic*, *Newsweek*, and the *New Yorker*—to a plethora of books that analyze various aspects of Obama's political rise and personal beliefs, Obama's relationship with Reverend Wright (and the black church generally) has not received the type of historical analysis that it warrants. Similarly, no sustained historical analysis has been presented to explain why Obama's mixed-race heritage and political rise truly are "historical."[29] Although analyses of Obama's religious beliefs and his relationship to Reverend Wright dominate the Obama literature, most of these accounts are journalistic and, as such, historically superficial.[30] Stephen Mansfield's *The Faith of Barack Obama* (2008), however, presents readers with the most thoughtful analysis of race and religion to date. Mansfield presents a nuanced analysis of Trinity United Church of Christ, the reasons for Obama joining the Trinity community, and Reverend Wright's preaching. As Mansfield argues of Wright, "To claim him crazy and dismiss him from the scene without a hearing is to miss an opportunity to heal a grievous, festering wound."[31] Indeed, Mansfield, like Wright and Obama, recognizes that black Americans experience race in ways of which white Americans are often willfully ignorant. Black ministers like Wright thus present an opportunity for genuine racial understanding, an opportunity that is so often drowned out by accusations of radical "rantings," unpatriotic preaching, and anti-white racism.[32]

This book provides heretofore absent historical perspective on race, religion, sexuality, and politics in the 2008 presidential election. In the first chapter, we argue that rather than being a "lunatic," as a number of vocal critics suggest, Reverend Wright belongs to an American tradition of preaching that dates back to the Puritans. Wright's preaching is in the tradition of what historians once called the black church—that is, of a black-run institution that is thought of in the singular, irrespective of how many Christian denominations exist in black America—that speaks to the spiritual needs of an urban black congregation. As a result, his sermons do not focus on the banal "feel-goodism" that characterizes so much contemporary white evangelicalism. Wright's preaching is political; he speaks to the historic injustices that black people have suffered in a republic that has been characterized by white supremacy. His preaching reflects, as the historian Nathan Irvin Huggins once remarked, that "the American dogma of automatic progress fails those who have been marginalized."[33] Wright, therefore, is not an anomaly; rather, we argue that he is a prominent spokesman of Black Theology of Liberation, a movement of black ministers that "presupposes that working people and the poor possess an active faith that inspires them to practice freedom as a major definition of what it means to be a full human being."[34] In twenty-first-century America, where the ideas associated with "postracialism" are gaining increasing support, the publicity surrounding Wright's sermons during 2008 raised the specter of a black radicalism that reminded us that American society has a way to go before it transcends its racial history.

In the second chapter, we turn to the issues of Obama's mixed-race heritage and his place in American political history since the Reconstruction era of the 1860s and 1870s. We analyze changing perceptions of racial mixture and discuss how Obama grappled with changing ideas about interracial sex and mixed-race identity. This historical analysis makes it possible to place Obama's significant contribution to American social and political life in a clearer historical perspective, something that is missing from previous books and articles on Obama's life. We also discuss the important history that Obama belongs to as a mixed-race politician. Guiding this analysis is the question of how Obama was able to overcome the weight of historically constructed stereotypes that, even in 2008, cast the "mulatto" politician as a shiftless, cunning, and corrupt figure.

Finally, we hope this little book will contribute to a clearer understanding of black Christianity in the lives of African Americans. The Wright incident, and the resulting intense media scrutiny of Obama's relationship with his former pastor, suggests that the United States has not yet overcome the greatest skeleton in its closet: *race*. Thomas Jefferson, the third president of the United States, once remarked that "slavery was like having 'the wolf by the ears: it is unjust to hold it, but it is unsafe to let it go.'"[35] Though Jefferson did not live long enough to see its demise, slavery did eventually end. And yet, the racial oppression of African American people has continued.[36] As the 2008 presidential campaign reminds us, racial stereotypes and injustice continue to impact the lives of millions of Americans, suggesting that America's real "wolf," race, remains on the loose. Irrespective of the coded language that is used to describe race in contemporary America, there are some among us who appear to still believe that "it is unsafe to let it go."

The "Chickens Are Coming Home to Roost"

Jeremiah Wright, Barack Obama, and the Black Church

The Reverend Jeremiah Wright, the former pastor of Trinity United Church of Christ on the South Side of Chicago, sparked outrage in large sections of the United States in February and March 2008, after the contents of his post-9/11 sermons were made public by Internet sites, the print media, and television news outlets. Wright's sermons, which can be found in selectively edited formats on the Internet site YouTube, depict the former Trinity pastor excoriating the United States for its historical injustices against racial minorities. In an oft-quoted sermon, Wright preaches that the United States "government gives them [blacks] the drugs, builds bigger prisons, passes a three-strike law and then wants us to sing 'God Bless America.' No, no, no, not God Bless America, God damn America, that's in the Bible for killing innocent people, God damn America for treating our [black] citizens as less than human."[1] The circulation of Wright's damnation of America sermon prompted immediate public outrage; letters of indignation and disgust flooded newspapers and Internet blogs. But Wright's sermon after the terrorist attacks on September 11, 2001, caused the most outrage among large segments of the American public. Wright sermonized that the

United States' support of both apartheid in South Africa and Israeli attacks on the Palestinians were just two examples of an aggressive and immoral foreign policy that had contributed to the rise of anti-American terrorism. "Now we are indignant because the stuff we have done overseas is now brought right back into our own backyard," Wright proclaimed; "America's chickens are coming home to roost."[2]

News media analysis of Wright's sermons turned the former pastor of Trinity United Church of Christ into a cause célèbre during the Democratic Party's primary election in February and March 2008. One of the Democratic candidates, Barack Obama, had for two decades been a member of Wright's Trinity community on the South Side of Chicago. The controversy surrounding Wright's sermons threatened to derail Obama's bid for the White House, prompting the then–presidential hopeful to disavow Wright's remarks and sever his ties with Trinity. The controversy surrounding Reverend Wright, and Barack Obama's association with the controversial pastor, shed light on the historic function of the black church in the United States. In this chapter, we will use the political controversy surrounding Wright's sermons to place Jeremiah Wright in the historical context of the black church in America. Our analysis will consider the historical importance of black preaching, and reveal the important role that the black church continues to play in providing political and social support networks for millions of black Americans. We will also assess the historical significance of Wright's Afrocentric statements concerning black history and Africa, statements that added fuel to the suspicions many white Americans harbor about preachers like Jeremiah Wright.

The Black Church in Historical Context

For Jeremiah Wright, as for so many black Americans, a sense of historical consciousness centers on the issues of racial slavery, Jim Crow segregation, and the day-to-day racism that remains part of contemporary American life. Forty-five years after the passage of the Civil Rights Act of 1964, black Americans still live with a history of discrimination. Although America has made tremendous progress in dealing with its racial problems, racism continues to alter the lives of large segments of the American population and define the terms on which racial and ethnic groups are meant to assimilate into a Western democracy like the United States. The contemporary emphasis on "postracialism" and "color blindness" is reminiscent of eighteenth- and nineteenth-century liberalism's offer to assimilate Europe's Jews, who were considered the classic "other" in European society, just as blacks have been in America. In the United States, as in Europe, liberalism has historically emphasized a quest for human progress through social cohesion. In Europe, for example, nineteenth-century demands for Jewish assimilation highlighted the ideological importance of social unity and cohesion to the ideal of human progress. The historian Shulamit Volkov argues that in Revolutionary France, Count Stanislas de Clermont-Tonnerre stood before the National Assembly in 1789 and declared, "To the Jews as individuals—everything; to the Jews as a group—nothing."[3] In a similar vein, Prussia's Heinrich von Treitschke insisted that the Jews "should become Germans, feel themselves simply and completely Germans."[4]

Black people in the United States can relate to these historical experiences; however, unlike the Jews of central and western Europe, African Americans have historically been marked as *black*, and as a result, their color, culture, and history (real and imagined) have worked against their assimilation into the mainstream of America's liberal society. In essence, black Americans have never been thought of as individuals, but rather as a predominantly inferior group, an assumption on which both slavery and Jim Crow were built. This begins to explain the significance attributed to Obama's relationship with Wright during the 2008 presidential campaign: Obama's racial identification as a black man inhibited his ability, in the minds of Reverend Wright's critics, to think as an individual. But before we delve into contemporary racial politics, further historical analysis of race and religion in America is required.

For more than two hundred years, the black church has provided African American people with the faith, strength, and social services needed to survive in a country that has enslaved them, discriminated against them, lynched them, and legally segregated them from white Americans. Against this historical backdrop of exploitation and injustice, the black church has remained, as one spiritual proclaims, "a rock in a weary land."[5] However, because the black church has been the wealthiest and most independent of black institutions, some white Americans have harbored suspicions about its true objectives. From the time that black ministers were suspected of inspiring slave rebellions, to the civil rights movement in the 1950s and 1960s, the black church and its clergy—men like Jeremiah Wright—have often struck fear into the hearts of white Americans by insisting that they are "speaking truth to power." Like the eighteenth- and nineteenth-century Quaker ministers, such as George Fox and the abolitionist Benjamin Lay, who mixed biblical prophecy—most notably from the prophet Jeremiah—with robust and exuberant performances to urge followers to fight social evils like slavery, black ministers often work within the Puritan tradition of the jeremiad, a type of sermon that has been adapted over the centuries to answer the needs of both black and white ministers.[6]

In the seventeenth century, the Puritans colonized and settled what is today New England. Puritan leaders used jeremiads to characterize what they believed was their new homeland's special relationship with God. In his 1630 sermon "A Model of Christian Charity," the Puritan divine John Winthrop instructed his coreligionists that "The eyes of all people are upon us. So that if we shall falsely deal with our God in this work we have undertaken, and so cause Him to withdraw his present help from us, we shall be made a story and a by word throughout the world . . . if our hearts shall turn away, so that we will not obey, but shall be seduced, and worship other Gods, our pleasure and profits, and serve them; it is propounded unto this day, we shall surely perish out of the good land whither we pass over this vast sea to possess it."[7] Winthrop's America was a covenanted society: failure to live up to God's expectations meant that the country would suffer God's wrath and divine retribution. The Puritan clergy, and the black preachers who later adopted a similar style of preaching, taught that whenever Zion sinned, God would punish the people.

Winthrop's jeremiad was designed to warn his people that they must rectify their shortcomings if they were to maintain their covenanted relationship with God. The prophet Jeremiah provided the inspiration for Winthrop's, and future generations', jeremiads. In the book of Lamentations, both Zion and Jerusalem are denounced for disobeying God, with the prophet Jeremiah declaring: "the Lord was an enemy: he hath swallowed up Israel, he hath swallowed up all of her palaces, he hath destroyed his strongholds" (Lam. 2:5–6). Jeremiah continues: "he hath violently taken away his tabernacle, as if it were a garden: he hath destroyed his places of assembly: the Lord has caused the solemn feast and Sabbaths to be forgotten in Zion, and hath despised in the indignation of his anger the King and the priest."[8] From the sermons of John Winthrop to those of Jeremiah Wright, the words of the prophet Jeremiah in the book of Lamentations have provided generations of black and white Americans with a recognizable trope with which to critique the United States' shortcomings. The trope of the jeremiad has undergone numerous changes since Winthrop settled with his coreligionists in New England, but by the time of the American Revolution in the 1770s, the sin of slavery was clearly in the sights of America's jeremiahs.

As the American people struggled to define what it meant to be an American in the 1770s and 1780s, there existed no of ministers who offered jeremiads against the sin of [illegible] society founded on the ideals of liberty and freedom, these men warned, will fall victim to God's wrath if it does not cleanse itself of slavery. As early as 1787, Samuel Hopkins, the white pastor of Newport, Rhode Island's First Congregational Church, chastened his fellow white countrymen for tolerating both slavery and the slave trade. Hopkins warned that the traffic in African slaves was a contradiction of Christian teachings and America's Revolutionary ideology. However, as the meaning of national identity and belonging narrowed in the 1790s, the universal ideals of freedom and equality became the sole domain of the white man. Hopkins saw these developments on the horizon in his 1787 sermon and cautioned that Americans could not flout God's will that all men are equal, lest they incur his wrath. According to Hopkins, Americans must immediately abandon their participation in the slave trade and repent their sins.[9]

There existed no greater sin than slavery during the Revolutionary period and early republic, and black Americans were among those at the forefront of condemning the institution. Between the 1770s and rise of Jacksonian democracy in the 1820s, black ministers and laymen delivered numerous jeremiads against the institution of slavery. Typical of the tenor and tone of these antislavery jeremiads was that of an anonymous black essayist in 1788. Writing under the pseudonym "Othello," the anonymous author declared that American slavery was "an outrage to Providence and an affront to divine majesty, who has given to man His Own peculiar image."[10] "Slavery," Othello asserted, "unquestionably should be abolished, particularly in this country; because it is inconsistent with the declared principles of the American Revolution."[11]

It was during the period of the early republic, when the American nation was in its infancy, that Richard Allen entered the annals of American religious history by becoming the first bishop of the African Methodist Episcopal (AME) Church. Founded in 1794, the AME Church was the first in what became a long line of black churches that would minister to the needs of America's black communities in the nineteenth and twentieth centuries. Allen was a vocal opponent of slavery, and in 1794 he offered his own jeremiad against the enslavement of his people. Entitled "Those Who Keep Slaves and Approve the Practice," Allen's jeremiad warned white Americans that God did not approve of slavery: "I do not wish to make you angry, but excite your attention to consider how hateful slavery is in the sight of that God, who hath destroyed kings and princes for their oppression of poor slaves. Pharaoh and his princes, with the posterity of King Saul, were destroyed by the protector and avenger of slaves."[12] Although Allen did not live to see the United States plunged into a bloody civil war in 1861, he nonetheless recognized that God would punish the United States for the sin of slavery.

No other group of Americans prophesied so clearly about an internecine war that might result from racial slavery as black Americans. Throughout the antebellum era, from the election of President Andrew Jackson in 1828 to the outbreak of the Civil War in 1861, black ministers and laymen drew on the book of Lamentations to offer their jeremiads against the sin of racial slavery. One of the most famous examples of this literature came from the pen of a northern free black. In 1829, *David Walker's Appeal* became part of what the historian Peter Hinks labels a "well-established tradition of black anti-slavery and religious oratory."[13] Walker, a committed black abolitionist, combined stirring allusions to the wrath of the "Creator" and the ideals embodied in the Declaration of Independence. Walker used these images to challenge white Americans to live up to their professed ideals and abolish slavery. With words that demonstrated Walker's keen sense of politics and understanding of history, he asked rhetorically: "Now, Americans I ask you cordially was your suffering under Great Britain, one hundreth [*sic*] part as cruel and tyrannical as you have rendered ours under you?"[14]

The sense of injustice that Walker expressed was shared by other black abolitionists and intensified during the Civil War.

Frederick Douglass, the leading black abolitionist in antebellum America, warned that if the United States' leaders did not abolish slavery, "a terrible retribution awaits us."[15] When Douglass received the news in 1861 that Fort Sumter had been fired on, thus beginning the Civil War, he rejoiced with the words, "God be praised."[16] As the war raged and Confederate fortunes turned for the worse after 1863, both black and white ministers sermonized that "God had punished the South for failing to do justice to its slaves."[17] Typical of such preaching was the 1863 warning by North Carolinian Calvin H. Wiley, a Presbyterian minister, that "God is now chastening the [southern portion of the] country for its sins in connection with slavery."[18] In addition to Frederick Douglass, many black abolitionists added their voices to this chorus criticizing in religious terms the injustices perpetrated against America's slaves. Unless the North fought the Civil War with the explicit intent of abolishing slavery, black abolitionists maintained, God would forever judge the American people harshly for the "sin of slavery."[19]

Before the fortunes of war turned in favor of the Union army in 1863, black preachers drew on the techniques of the jeremiad to explain the North's military defeats. For example, the *Christian Recorder*, the official newspaper of the AME Church, excoriated the North for wanting to free the slaves only as a "military necessity" to preserve the Union.[20] When President Lincoln issued the Emancipation Proclamation and made slavery the central issue of the war after 1863, both black and white ministers saw God's punishment in the rapid decline and defeat of the South. These themes were also a part of President Lincoln's Second Inaugural Address:

> If we shall suppose that American slavery is one of those offenses which, in the providence of God, must needs come, but which, having continued through His appointed time, He now wills to remove, and that He gives to both North and South, this terrible war, as the woe due to those by

> whom the offense came, shall we discern therein any departure from those divine attributes which the believers in a Living God always ascribe to Him? Fondly do we hope—fervently do we pray—that this mighty scourge of war may speedily pass away. Yet, if God wills that it continue, until all wealth piled by the bond-man's two hundred and fifty years of un-repentant toil shall be sunk and until every drop of blood drawn with the lash, shall be paid by another drawn with the sword, as was said three thousand years ago, so still it must be said "the judgements of the Lord, are true and righteous altogether."[21]

For African Americans, the black church not only offered damning critiques of the sin of slavery, but provided a place of refuge from slavery, and from the white world more generally. For much of the nineteenth century, however, finding a refuge from slavery and a sympathetic minister to soothe one's spiritual pains was no easy task. During slavery, free blacks and slaves were often compelled to worship in white churches, where they were confined to segregated sections of the church known as "nigger pews," "heavens," or "servants' galleries." Restricted to these marginalized places of worship, blacks listened to white pastors instruct congregants on the importance of obeying one's master. The presence of white men in these services operated as a control mechanism through which white masters, overseers, and ministers attempted to ensure that nothing critical was said of slavery.[22]

White preachers in the slave South instructed slaves to accept their enslavement, be obedient to their masters and mistresses, and not steal the master's property. One former slave recalled: "When the white preacher come he preached and pick up his bible and he claim he gitten the text right out of the good book and he preached: 'the Lord say, don't you niggers steal chickens from your missus. Don't you steal your master's hawgs.' That would be all he preach."[23] Commenting on the desire of the slaves to transcend the limitations of white sermons, another slave observed, "the whites preached to the niggers and the niggers preached to themselves."[24] Preaching to themselves, the slaves developed a rich tradition of biblical oratory that led to the creation of a sermonic style rich in simile and metaphor that was based on the tales of the Jews in the Old Testament. Anyone familiar with the lyrics of black American spirituals will know that they depict black people as a chosen people. Black spirituals identify blacks as the "de people born of God"; "we are de people of de Lord"; "I am born of God, I know I am."[25] If Egypt was a land of travail for the Hebrew children, the United States had offered enslaved blacks an analogous sojourn.

For slaves who lived in the countryside or on large plantations, clandestine religious meetings offered an opportunity to develop a uniquely black American Christianity. Slaves held religious meetings at night in an effort to avoid the master's gaze. These black places of worship became known as "brush arbors." The sociologist E. Franklin Frazier has noted that these secret meetings were conducted away from the prying eyes of the slave master and his overseers.[26] Frazier argued that because slaves were dissatisfied with the religious instruction they received from their masters, they created the "invisible institution" of slave Christianity. This "invisible institution" formed the foundations of organized black churches, such as Allen's AME Church, in the United States.[27]

While divisions based on skin color, class, and religious denomination have existed among black Christians in America, it is important to understand that as slave religion developed in the South, free blacks in the North also found white Christianity to be deficient. This was why Richard Allen organized the AME Church in Philadelphia in 1794; it is also why other black churches sprang up throughout the North prior to the Civil War. These churches offered free blacks a place of worship, communal bonds, and financial support in times of hardship.[28] White Americans were immediately troubled by the emergence of black churches; they worried that black ministers preached against slavery. Proslavery advocates also accused black churches of aiding runaway slaves. As a result, whites policed black churches in both the North and South, often using terrorism and violence to intimidate black abolitionist ministers.[29]

Prior to the Civil War, black churches in the North led opposition to proposals that freed African Americans be transported back to Africa. The American Colonization Society championed the cause of transporting freed blacks to Africa. The black churches in the North vehemently rejected such schemes, and instead urged their congregants to cultivate "progress toward 'respectable' life."[30] Black churches in antebellum America raised money that they expended on the development of their church community, thereby creating a space in which black Americans could express pride. Displays of such pride rankled northern whites. In 1830, a white Philadelphia historian wrote disdainfully of black values and aspirations:

> In the olden time, dressy blacks and dandy colored beaux and belles, as we see them issuing from their proper churches, were quite unknown. Their aspiring and little known vanities have been growing since they got those separate churches. Once they submitted to the appellation of servants, blacks, or negroes, but now they require to be called coloured people, and among themselves, their common call of salutation is—gentlemen and ladies.[31]

Such statements highlight the anxiety that northern whites felt about black success. Moreover, it was the fear that blacks were plotting political or social activism that made black churches and their ministers the targets of white suspicion during the antebellum era and beyond.[32] The 2008 controversy over Reverend Jeremiah Wright's sermons suggests that while black churches throughout the United States continue to act as centers of political and social activity, they are also sites on which the racial anxieties of some white Americans remain focused.

Jeremiah Wright and the Black Church

Who, then, is the Reverend Jeremiah Wright, and how does he fit into this history of the black church? Before he was plunged into the media spotlight in February and March 2008 for his sermons and his connection with Barack Obama, Wright had been a prominent black minister on the South Side of Chicago who had the respect of the members of his denomination, the United Church of Christ. Indeed, everyone who knew Wright appreciated his socially conscious and activist ministry. But before he established this ministry, Wright had followed a relatively typical middle-class American path from childhood to educational accomplishment and positions of social responsibility.

Wright was not born in a ghetto, but grew up in a mixed-raced neighborhood in Germantown, a suburb of Philadelphia. His father was the minister of the Grace Baptist Church, where he ministered to Germantown blacks for forty-two years. Wright's mother was a schoolteacher who went on to become the vice principal of Germantown Girls High School. Wright's parents enrolled their son in the well-regarded, integrated Central High School of Philadelphia, where 90 percent of the student body was white. A description of Wright in his class yearbook reads, "Always ready with a kind word, Jerry is one of the most congenial members of the 211." Unlike some black teenagers in integrated high schools, Wright was not popular because he was an athlete, a good dancer, or a cheerleader; instead, Wright's "record in Central is a model for lower class [younger] members to emulate," the class annual proclaimed. If Wright is bitter, as his critics suggest, his anger is not the product of a disadvantaged black childhood.

After graduating from Central High School, Wright studied at Virginia Union University between 1959 and 1961. He left the university to become a marine, and then joined the United States Navy, serving in the medical corps. The highlight of his service came in 1966 when he was part of the medical team that cared for President Lyndon Johnson after his surgery. After leaving the military in 1967, Wright studied at Howard University in Washington, D.C., where he earned both a bachelor's and master's degree. Wright next moved to Chicago, where he enrolled in the Divinity School of the University of Chicago, ultimately earning another master's degree. Wright completed his education by studying for a doctor of ministry at the United Theological Seminary in Dayton, Ohio, where he came under the tutelage of Samuel DeWitt Proctor, who had taught Martin Luther King Jr.[33]

Wright belongs to a predominantly white denomination, the United Church of Christ. The United Church of Christ has its origins in Puritan New England, situating the church in the reform tradition of American Protestantism. Wright, however, is a practitioner of Black Theology of Liberation, something that press coverage about Wright was at pains to emphasize. Black Theology of Liberation is a Christian movement that was created by a group of black ministers in the late 1960s. The leaders of this movement believed that the teachings of Jesus Christ contained a positive message for black people, despite the racism that they encountered from white Christian Americans. Although Black Theology of Liberation is often associated with Professor James Cone, who in 1969 published the influential book *Black Theology and Black Power,* and later *A Black Theology of Liberation* (1970), important ideas of Black Theology of Liberation date back to the eighteenth century. In particular, the notion that "Christ called for a ministry in which God and human beings would work together to transform . . . oppressive social [conditions] into a new Community of Justice on earth" featured prominently in eighteenth- and nineteenth-century black theology, as it did in Black Theology of Liberation after the 1960s.[34] Wright's theological outlook, and his ministry in general, therefore drew from a multiracial Christian heritage to address the spiritual and social needs of his black congregants at Trinity.

Wright's historical consciousness is also indebted to the multiracial religious influences in his life. These religious influences, coming from both white and black interpretations of Christianity, have meant that Wright has felt duty-bound to address the historical and contemporary injustice that shapes the lives of his congregants. Contrary to his critics' claims that Wright's remarks about American history are a version of the 1970s variety program *The Gong Show*, or "inflammatory," "incendiary," or "unpatriotic,"[35] Wright's preaching is part of a tradition, as we have shown, that dates back to the seventeenth century, when both black and white ministers damned America for its failings.[36] Like ministers who delivered jeremiads to seventeenth- and eighteenth-century congregations, Wright warns in his sermons that God's wrath will be incurred if social injustices are not addressed. However, Wright's sermons are also prepared specifically for a black audience struggling with inner-city life in contemporary America.

Wright's remarks about America's past, and its present, represent an American tradition in which the United States' liberal mythology of independence, human progress, and equality of opportunity is challenged.[37] Wright has not necessarily sought to undermine these values; rather, he has challenged all Americans to make them a lived reality for the black Americans on the South Side of Chicago to whom he ministers. One of Wright's most famous sermons, "The Day of Jerusalem's Fall," speaks to the darker elements of America's colonial past, a history often forgotten or romanticized in the liberal version of American progress, or in the Disney version of history. In "The Day of Jerusalem's Fall," Wright observes that the United States' colonial origins were characterized by the dispossession and killing of Native American peoples. In Wright's words, "We took this country by terror away from the Sioux, the Apache, Arikara, the Comanche, the Arapaho."[38] This aspect of American history is something that most Americans prefer to forget, but that Wright has not forgotten. Nor has Wright forgotten that the economic prosperity that is such an important aspect of the United States' master narrative was built on the backs of African slaves. Wright stated, "We took the Africans from their country to build our way of ease and kept them enslaved and living in fear."[39] It would be a mistake to think that Wright is alone among black Americans in this understanding of American history. Jerome Smith, a former civil rights Freedom Rider, told David Remnick, the editor of the *New Yorker,* that "Obama's minister did not lie when he said that the controlling power in this country was rich white men. Rich white men were responsible for slavery. They are responsible for unspeakable levels of poverty for African Americans."[40] Being aware of this history and how it continues to impact the lives of thousands of Americans is to confront the fact that America is not the exceptional "City on a Hill" that the Disney version of American history portrays.[41] In fact, "The Day of Jerusalem's Fall" acknowledges that the United States was part of a worldwide process of European imperial expansion, colonization, dispossession, genocide, and enslavement.[42]

When these remarks were made public in February and March 2008, they angered millions of Americans; millions more expressed outrage over claims that were roundly dismissed as the rantings of a conspiracy theorist. Wright's assertion that the United States "government gives them [blacks] the drugs" is an accusation that continues to be part of the black urban rumor mill. Black Americans have made these accusations and others, such as that Jewish doctors have been infecting African Americans with AIDS, for decades, if not centuries. Such claims are made in the context of a historical consciousness in which racial slavery, Jim Crow segregation, and political powerlessness are important themes. In his 1995 memoir, *Dreams from My Father,* Barack Obama dismissed conspiracy theories that "Jewish doctors were injecting black babies with the AIDS virus."[43] Obama's dismissal of these conspiracy theories is perhaps a reflection of his not having grown up as the grandchild of slaves, or as the son of parents who had been victims of Jim Crow in the South. Among such Americans, as among other oppressed groups around the world—such as the Armenians who were slaughtered by the Ottoman Turks or the Jews killed by the Nazis—conspiracy theories are a common response to having endured generations of oppression and historical injustice.[44]

The long history of medical experimentation on African Americans in the United States is part of black historical consciousness. For example, Thomas Jefferson, the author of the Declaration of Independence and the third president of the United States, experimented on his slaves in an attempt to find a cure for smallpox.[45] Before the Civil War, the slave John Brown reported that his master, trying to find a cure for sunstroke, allowed a doctor to suspend him in a charcoal-filled pit that was covered with wet blankets.[46] J. Marion Simms's gynecological operations on the slave girls Anarcha, Betsy, and Lucy were perhaps the most outrageous experiments conducted on blacks in antebellum America. Simms operated on Anarcha more than thirty times in an effort to correct a vesicovaginal fistula. Simms did not administer anesthesia to any of his patients until he completed his operations. Like other white doctors who treated slaves, Simms believed that blacks had a higher tolerance for pain than whites, making them perfect test subjects for medical experiments.[47]

In his childhood, Wright no doubt heard horrendous stories about the 1929 Tuskegee Syphilis Study. The Tuskegee study involved black men being admitted to a government veterans' hospital where they were not treated for syphilis because, as medical professionals informed them, they had "bad blood."[48] Tuskegee was not an isolated incident. In the 1930s, the North Carolina Eugenics Commission sterilized eight thousand mentally retarded persons, five thousand of whom were black.[49]

Since medical experimentation on black people is part of the black American historical memory, it is glib and insensitive to dismiss Wright as a crank and conspiracy theorist for making similar claims. Indeed, how does one distinguish between paranoia and social policy when the future first lady Michelle Obama, in her capacity as the president of community affairs at the University of Chicago's Medical Center in 2001, was forced to prevent doctors working on the papillomavirus vaccine from contacting high school principals with a request to perform experiments on Chicago's black teenage girls?[50]

If Wright has appropriated the Puritan jeremiad and the Quaker tradition of "speaking truth to power" to critique America's racial failings, he has also adapted the reforming ethos of the United Church of Christ and the message of black pride and "chosen-ness" in Black Theology of Liberation. Like thousands of black preachers before him, Wright uses the biblical story of Jewish captivity in Babylon as a metaphor for the African American experience in the United States. In his sermon "Faith in a Foreign Land," Wright uses the story of Jewish captives in Babylon to explain what he sees as the deracination of contemporary black Americans:

> The North American slave owners, those "Babylonians," prototypes of the empire and the imperialistic mind-set that disregards anything everybody else has ever done, did away with the natives' names in an attempt to take away their history. . . . They lost their history, so they died. Our children don't know our story. Any people who lose their story are a dead people. And the established authority, the empire, knows that, so it makes every deliberate attempt to take away the exiles' history. The empire tells them that they have no history prior to the Babylonians introducing them to civilization; the empire tells them outright lies and blatant distortions so that they will disown any linkage that

> they once had with Africa, and they become more Babylonian than the Babylonians.[51]

Wright's homily has its origins in the history of slavery and in the Afrocentric interpretation of black American history. We will have more to say about Wright's reading of the black past in our conclusion. What is important to note here is that the Afrocentric misunderstanding of slavery and its cultural consequence is matched by the determination of many white Americans to view slavery as a long-forgotten mistake of the past, and this explains the hysteria and utter lack of public empathy for Reverend Wright's preaching.

Wright's adherence to the ideals of black Christian nationalism also sparked controversy during 2008. In the 1960s, Black Theology of Liberation breathed new vigor into black Christian nationalism, a tradition grounded in an older belief that the black church is "politically and socially relevant to the lives of black people."[52] This tradition has historically been held together by the idea that "the poor and the oppressed occupy a special place in God's eye."[53] The theologian Dwight N. Hopkins calls this religious practice "the Preferential Option for the Poor and the Oppressed":

> To prefer a specific option for working people and growing communities sinking into a system of poverty puts love of neighbor above private accumulation of things. It cuts across the grain of everything that instantaneous gratification and a commodified, consumer economy demand. In the global arena, with the United States representing the sole international super power, we might conclude that to resist the seduction of the "American way of life" appears futile. But the preferential option for the poor serves as a spiritual calling to redefine our humanity based not on our individual possessions but on serving people who struggle to attain basic material and spiritual possessions. More specifically, the humanity of the privileged elite at the top

> of society arises from a recognition of the humanity of the vast non-wealthy group at the bottom of society.[54]

The kind of socially activist Christianity embodied in "the Preferential Option for the Poor and the Oppressed" emphasizes helping the dispossessed. This stands in sharp contrast to the Word of Faith movement, which is also known as "Faith-Formula," "Hyper-Faith," "Name It and Claim It," and "Health, Wealth, and Prosperity Teaching." The Word of Faith movement teaches that it is "God's will for Christians to be prosperous, successful, and healthy."[55] Based on a degraded form of nineteenth-century Protestantism called "mind cure," Word of Faith lacks the political edge of the Christianity preached by Jeremiah Wright.[56] Word of Faith has been more popular among white Americans because it does not challenge the American myth of individual success. Moreover, Word of Faith is often used to instruct white people that there is no racism or race problem in the United States. If black people are poor and disadvantaged, it is because they have chosen impoverishment. This is the new "Balm of Gilead" in a neoliberal age. Wright's criticism of America, as we have noted, is rooted in Black Theology of Liberation and black Christian nationalism that rejects the Word of Faith movement and urges black people to forge a model of faith different from white evangelical Christianity.

Jeremiah Wright and the parishioners to whom he ministers are not what the historian Alan Taylor calls "conspicuous Christians."[57] For millions of Americans, Taylor argues, Christianity has become more of a slogan—much like a pithy motivational mantra emblazoned across a T-shirt—than a deep, living faith. Mark Noll, a prominent evangelical and a scholar of American Protestantism, has discussed this religious development in a work entitled *The Scandal of the Evangelical Mind.* Noting that earlier generations of evangelicals had been intellectually rigorous, Noll argues that "none of them believed that intellectual activity was the only way to glorify God, or even the highest way, but they all believed in it *because* they were evangelical Christians."[58]

Noll's analysis is a timely reminder of how historical amnesia is as dangerous to the Christian believer as it is to the nonbeliever. This historical amnesia was on display at the 2008 Republican National Convention. When Sarah Palin, the Alaska governor and Republican Party nominee for vice president, mocked Barack Obama's intellectual curiosity and belittled his "community organizing," she forgot that a close reading of the Bible would reveal that Jesus himself was a community organizer ministering to the poor and dispossessed of Palestine. In other words, Jesus ministered to people who were oppressed by the "Evil Empire" of his day: the Roman Empire. Unlike Palin, black people like Jeremiah Wright and Barack Obama have not forgotten the social work performed by Jesus and recognize that this aspect of Christianity must remain a central tenet of their faith.

Jeremiah Wright inherited black Christian nationalism, Black Theology of Liberation, and the black church's social activism from a long lineage of African American ministers who believed that white interpretations of Christianity had failed the people they represented.[59] The AME Church and the African Methodist Episcopal Zion Church (founded in 1796) have provided ministers such as Wright with the starting point from which to develop black Christian nationalism and instill pride and self-respect in generations of black Christians in America.[60] For example, the nineteenth-century AME bishop Henry M. Turner stopped a church conference from singing the hymn "Wash Me and I Shall Be Whiter than Snow," angrily telling the meeting: "That's the trouble with colored folk now. You just want to be white. Quit singing that song and quit trying to be white. The time has come when we must be proud that we are black and proud of our race."[61] Turner's act offers an example of how black ministers have endeavored to transform the black psyche and make black people proud of themselves. Turner suggested here that a white-centered Christianity cultivated a sense of racial inferiority among black Americans. To counteract such feelings, Turner told his people that "God is a Negro."[62]

Turner's proclamation of God's blackness challenged the Anglo-American depiction of Jesus as a white man. From the rise of Christianity to the nineteenth century, every race of people has created God in their image. Turner's black God was a classic example of black Christian nationalism; it was also his way of telling black people that whites had constructed God in their image. As Turner put it, God was not "a white-skinned blue-eyed, projecting-nosed, compressed-lipped and finely robed *white* gentleman, sitting on a throne somewhere in the heavens."[63] Turner thus anticipated future black Christian nationalist depictions of Jesus and the Apostles as black. Such depictions of Jesus and the disciples can be seen in the Trinity United Church of Christ, as in other black churches throughout America. For more than two hundred years, these black sanctuaries have depicted Jesus and his disciples as black in the stained-glass windows of the church. And before the advent of air-conditioning in the South, pictures on the hand-held church fans that black congregants used to cool themselves during services depicted biblical scenes in which the Apostles and Christ were black.[64] This religious iconography was not—and is not—wishful thinking on the part of black ministers like Turner and Wright. Instead, these depictions represented an understanding that many of the people in the Bible were not the white people so often portrayed in American cinema and Christian iconography.[65] More importantly, these images demonstrate the independence of mind and spirit of American blacks, and their desire to take possession of their own forms of worship, all of which continues to trouble white Americans.

Wright's efforts to instill pride in African American people have often seen him address issues of gender as well as race. Aware of the negative and emasculating effects that slavery, Jim Crow segregation and lynching, lack of education, and under-employment as well as unemployment have historically had on the black male psyche, Wright has often focused on the self-esteem of black men. In his sermon "What Makes You So Strong?" Wright celebrates black American men's strength in the face of an omnipresent white racism:

> How is it that after all this country has done to you, you can still produce a Paul Robeson, a Thurgood Marshall, a Malcolm X (el-Hajj Malik el-Shabazz), a Martin King, and a Ron McNair? What makes you so strong, black man?
>
> This country has tried castration and lynching, mis-education and brain-washing. They have taught you to hate yourself and to look at yourself through the awfully tainted eyeglasses of white Eurocentric lies, and yet you keep breaking out of the prisons they put you in. You break out in a W. E. B. Du Bois and a Booker T. Washington; you break out in a Louis Farrakhan and a Mickey Leland; you break out in a Judge Thurgood Marshall and a Pops Staples; you break out in a Luther Vandross, Magic Johnson, Michael Jordan, Harold Washington, or a Doug Wilder. What makes you so strong, black man?[66]

Wright here mixes black Christian nationalism, Black Theology of Liberation, and an African American political tradition of emphasizing the importance of black manhood. In antebellum America, for example, the African American abolitionist Frederick Douglass repeatedly criticized the United States for the manner in which it denied black men their manhood. Douglass emphasized that "every page [of American history] is red with the blood of the American slavery," and yet, despite this, black men were forming political and religious associations devoted to "equal and exact justice" for the black man.[67] Like Douglass before him, Wright understands that black men—and, indeed, black women—must overcome great obstacles to accomplish any measure of success in the United States.

Wright's sermons are part of a long tradition of preaching in the United States that mixes social commentary, scriptural citations, and political activism. Wright's words—be they the often-quoted "God damn America," or "America's chickens are coming home to roost"—are not anti-American, unpatriotic, or even radical sentiments, but are instead words rich in religious and political meaning that draw from a deep well of Christian activism in the American colonies and the United States. Wright's sermons are part of a tradition of communitarian survival. Not intended for a YouTube audience, these homilies are directed to black people and are designed to let the "folk" know, as the hymn says, that their "living will not be in vain," that black life has a purpose. They ask blacks to stand up and bear witness when they think their country has done wrong. Wright, like Martin Luther King Jr., wants to "make of this old world a new world." In this sense, Wright is as socially conscious and patriotic an American as any other citizen—black or white—of the United States.

Jeremiah Wright in a "Postracial" America

So why, then, did Wright become such a controversial part of the 2008 presidential election? Why, as some critics argued, did he threaten to derail Barack Obama's bid for the Oval Office? A large part of the answer to these questions rests on acknowledging that the black Christianity that Wright and millions of other African Americans practice decenters whiteness as normative to Christian identity and religious practice. Whiteness as the norm is at the core of modern definitions of "postracialism" and "color blindness," and those espousing these notions therefore deem assertive, self-respecting, proud blackness to be extremely threatening to social cohesion in the United States. Indeed, in historical and contemporary terms, all forms of black nationalists—be they black Christian nationalists, Muslims, Afrocentrists, or black secularists—insist that the people they represent must be liberated from the psychological domination of whiteness, or, in modern parlance, "postracialism."[68] In reality, the modern notions of "postrace" America and "color blindness" demand that black Americans shed their black skin—perhaps in a skin-whitening machine, as the black novelist George Schuyler sardonically wrote in 1931—and become white, that is, postracial.[69] Wright refuses to accept such ideologies, as did his predecessor at Trinity, Dr. Reuben Sheares, whose motto for the church was: "Unashamedly Black."[70] Wright has thus refused to play the role of preacher accomodationist, something that millions of white Americans find deeply troubling.[71]

Postracialism, like postnationalism and "color blindness," suggests that the world's people have moved beyond racial subjectivity and group identity. However, as we suggested in the introduction, being anti-identity is to have an identity. In the United States, that identity has historically been colored (biologically and culturally) white. This basic understanding of American racial history and its continuing impact on contemporary race relations was missed by Shelby Steele in his recent *A Bound Man* (2008). Steele imagines a raceless society, arguing that "what people really want to know is what it is like to have no race to go home to at night."[72] But do all Americans really want this? After all, to be anti-identity is to ignore the historically constructed gendered, racial, political, and sexual identities that give meaning to life. To erase these multiple and interconnected identities from American life would require a radical rewriting—or, as is more common, a forgetting—of American history. As the anthropologist Audrey Smedley has argued, "there is a reality to the idea of race that is grounded in our historical consciousness and in all of our political, economic, religious, recreational, and social institutions."[73]

Shelby Steele's use of clever phraseology glosses over a basic tenet of American history: that "everyone in this social order [in the United States] has been constructed in our political imagination as a racialised subject."[74] Steele, like other proponents of a "postracial" or "color-blind" America, argues that the United States is in the midst of a period of racial mixture that is helping to eliminate the racial categories that once divided white and black Americans. The United States, from its colonial origins to the present, has always been a racially mixed nation, something that has not prevented bitter racial tensions or the political, legal, and social policing of a white/nonwhite racial binary in American history.[75] During 2008, the controversy caused by Wright's sermons and his twenty-year relationship with Barack Obama highlighted the continued importance of race in structuring American life and shaping the collective historical consciousness of black and white Americans.[76] In a "society historically organized," as the historian Manning Marable observes, "around structural racism," people from historically oppressed groups have memories that distinguish them from their oppressors.[77] And since race and racial memories have been a central component of American society, to destroy these memories would require a fundamental reinvention of the "country, the social order, [and] the government."[78]

Wright has demonstrated an awareness that the history of blacks has not made the American republic *e pluribus unum*, a nation where all racial and ethnic differences are assimilated into a comfortable and harmonious whole.[79] Wright, like the nineteenth-century abolitionist William Lloyd Garrison, is a Christian moralist who places his moral beliefs above patriotism. Wright's critics failed to recognize this historically informed aspect of his ministry, wanting Wright to instead be a self-censoring patriot. Implicit in some Americans' criticism of Wright was the desire to silence this articulate black minister, lest he remind all that black history is a tale of a marginalized and oppressed people. In other words, Wright "reminds many whites," as the *Economist* observed in May 2008, "of everything they find alarming about black Americans."[80] This anxiety is more complicated than the quotation from the *Economist* suggests. For white Americans to recognize the reality of black history requires a level of self-consciousness about the American racial past that many whites resist comprehending.

Wright insisted in his sermons that black Americans maintain a strong sense of identity. In a sermon entitled "When You Forget Who You Are," Wright articulates the importance of identity to black Americans. This sermon is based on the story of Queen Esther in Babylon. In one section of the sermon, called "Esther Forgot Who She Was," Wright expresses his nationalist sensibilities. Wright does this in the context of modern ideas about racial assimilation, claiming, "when you assimilate you forget who you are."[81] This sermon is a cautionary tale about being black in America and the perils of losing one's self in the dominant culture. However, as we demonstrate in the final section of this chapter, some of Wright's arguments are historically problematic.

What millions of white Americans seem to find frightening about Wright is his apparent anger and the potential for this anger to spill over into social unrest, thereby disrupting the tidy "postracial" narrative that is currently taking shape in America. The late James Baldwin accurately labeled as rage what whites perceive to be black anger. Baldwin described black America's rage for the historical injustices perpetrated against their ancestors in these terms:

> I first contracted some dread, chronic disease, the unfurling of which is a kind of blind fever, a pounding in the skull and fire in the bowels. Once this disease is contracted one can never be really carefree again, for the fever, without an instant's warning, can recur at any moment. It can wreck more important things than race relations. There is not a Negro alive who does not have this rage in his blood—one has the choice of living with it consciously or surrendering to it.[82]

Baldwin may have been exaggerating when he claimed that all blacks "have this rage in [their] blood." But even if most blacks do not feel "rage" or "anger," they are certainly skeptical about the promise of American life, liberty, and the pursuit of happiness. Black history in the United States warrants this frame of mind, something that Wright's post-9/11 sermons captured. Minorities do not have the privilege of being completely uncritical of the societies in which they live. In most predominantly white countries with nonwhite citizens, racial and ethnic minorities encounter daily reminders that they are outsiders.[83]

The national mythology of the United States being an inclusive land of opportunity has been perpetuated by the Disney version of American history. From movie remakes of the story of Pocahontas's "love affair" with the Englishman John Smith, to films that reinforce American ideals of individualism and social harmony over the reality of colonial violence and the dispossession of Native Americans, to fanciful cinematic histories—such as *Song of the South* (1946)—of happy, contented slaves,[84] films shape and reshape how Americans forget their history. Indeed, the power of the Disney version of American history, especially in a "postracial" age, is that critics of American racial injustice like Reverend Wright are unthinkingly dismissed as angry and out of step with modern American society.

White Americans who expressed dismay over Wright's sermons grounded their criticisms in an unexamined pop-culture interpretation of American history. Such a history leaves many in white America suspicious of what African Americans really think. It remains an unfortunate truth that black America remains a frightening mystery to some white Americans. The historical segregation that has defined black and white church services goes a long way to explaining this phenomenon. Reverend Martin Luther King Jr. once remarked on this segregation—and the mutual ignorance that it breeds—when he said, "it is one of the tragedies of our nation, one of the shameful tragedies, that eleven o'clock on Sunday morning is the most segregated hour . . . in Christian America."[85] As most white Americans have little idea of what blacks discuss during Sunday morning church services, they are often shocked when sermons from the black pulpit reach the "mainstream" media. For example, very little discussion occurred during the 2008 presidential campaign over the fact that black "Americans have been the single most anti-war group in the population."[86] Knowledge of such statistics would likely send Wright's detractors into a paroxysm of fear, anger, and bewilderment at the lack of patriotism among black Americans. In truth, black Americans, as Wright expressed it in his post-9/11 speech, are historically aware that foreign policy decisions are not without their long-term consequences.

When Reverend Wright proclaimed after the 9/11 attacks that "America's chickens are coming home to roost," he opened a door to memories that white Americans have of "radical" black activists in the 1950s and 1960s.[87] Wright borrowed this phrase from the late Malcolm X, the black Muslim leader whom white Americans in the 1950s and 1960s saw as the embodiment of black militancy. But Wright, like Malcolm before him, knows what it means to view American history as an outsider from within. Malcolm X said it this way:

> No, I am not an American. I am one of the 22 million black people who are the victims of Americanism. One of the 22 million black people who are the victims of democracy, nothing but disguised hypocrisy. So I am not standing here speaking to you as an American, or a patriot, or a flag saluter, or a flag waver—no, not I. I'm speaking as a victim of this American system. And I see America through the eyes of the victim.[88]

Malcolm, like Wright, refused to offer unexamined encomiums to white America about its history of freedom, democracy, and equal opportunity; instead, both Malcolm and Wright belong to a long tradition of African American orators who have denounced American whiteness and railed against the hypocrisy of the United States' ideals.

The 2008 controversy over Reverend Wright's sermons reminded Americans of the uncomfortable fact that race remains the central social fissure in the United States.[89] Young African Americans live with the reality of race on a daily basis. For example, Michella Minter, a twenty-one-year-old black student in Huntington, West Virginia, expressed her sense that "people hate black people":

> I'm not trying to be racist or over the top, but it is seriously apparent that black people aren't valued in this country. In the last 12 months, six kids were being tried for attempted murder for a school fight, an unarmed man got 51 bullets in his body by a New York police officer, died, and no one was charged, and endless other racist unknown acts have occurred this year.[90]

Minter's views reflect the perceptions of many young black people. Wright recognizes that these racial perceptions continue to structure the lives of many black Americans; his sermons, therefore, are designed to minister to their continuing sense of racial marginality and feelings of inadequacy.

The language used by Wright, and Malcolm X before him, is not uncommon in black churches throughout the United States. Martin Peretz, the editor of the *New Republic*, observed that "the typical black church service is not a Unitarian prayer meeting or Catholic devotions. It is something 'other' that many of us have not experienced and do not know. It is not ours but theirs. And what's wrong with that?"[91] Peretz acknowledges that the black church and the preaching of its ministers is different, not deficient. The real issue to emerge out of the 2008 controversy over Wright's remarks is that when black Americans in positions of authority criticize the United States and its history, some white Americans respond by tarring all black leaders with the brush of black militancy. For a number of white Americans, the perception that Obama had intimate ties with a black militant leader like Wright called into question the so-called "new departure" in American politics, that is, the belief that contemporary black politicians are leaving behind the ways of those perceived as "in yo face Negroes" like Malcolm X, Al Sharpton, and Jesse Jackson.[92]

Critics of Wright's sermons expressed outrage over his remarks. Typical of these responses, one correspondent to a *New York Times* blog, claiming to speak for "normal white folks," combined historical amnesia, the mythology of American freedom, and its associated color blindness in her argument that Wright had cost Obama any chance of winning the presidential election:

> I believe we are now tired of hearing Wright and his throaty ravings . . . We the public {normal white folks} don't need to be schooled as he calls it.. He needs to come into the real world and quit blaming our forefathers and be thankful to be a free American.. Our generation had absolutely nothing to do with slavery and we are continually verbally punished by radical, bitter people like Wright. . . . He has killed any hope Obama ever had of becoming President. This legacy will follow him thru history . . . Thanks Wright. You have managed to RAVE the Democratic party to lose to McCain unless you can talk your protegee' Obama into pulling his name out of the race . . . He will never be President.[93]

Responses of this nature reflect the continuing power of race in America; because Obama had been a member of Trinity, this blogger assumes that he passively agreed with everything Wright said. In a supposedly "postracial" age, it is telling that some Americans cling to older racial ideologies that have all black Americans thinking alike.

Since the civil rights movement in the 1950s and 1960s, there has been a popular desire in many parts of white America to believe that the country has moved beyond race. The blogger quoted above reflects this mentality, in which any mention of race or racial injustice is likely to provoke a negative, sometimes hostile, reaction. This helps us to understand why

Wright's version of American history proved unsettling to some Americans, particularly those who subscribe to the belief that we have entered a "postracial" era in American history. Faith in the emergence of a "postracial" America has profound political implications for African Americans who run for public office. For example, Matt Bai, a columnist for the *New York Times*, gives voice to this idea in an article entitled "Is Obama the End of Black Politics?"[94] Bai argues that "for a lot of younger African-Americans, the resistance of the civil rights generation to Obama's candidacy signified the failure of their parents to come to terms, at the dusk of their lives, with the success of their own struggle—to embrace the idea that black politics might now be disappearing into American politics the same way that Irish and Italian machines long ago joined the political mainstream."[95]

Bai's piece represents a paean to the new generation of "coluhd politicians." He overlooks, however, that black politics would have become normative earlier if white ethnics had not blocked black Americans from entering mainstream politics.[96] Because Bai's focus is on national politics, he also fails to note that most black political activity takes place on the local level, and that local politics tends to be more insurgent. It is this political activity that so haunts white political memory. Both historians and sociologists have shown that black politics in the post-1964 United States was a reaction to white unease about the black liberation movement. Black anger, in public opinion, was disassociated from structural racism. Black anger was an indication that black people did not understand the American way. This assumption, coming in the wake of the Civil Rights Act of 1964 and the Voting Rights Act of 1965, reflected a desire on the part of America's white majority to think that the "race problem" had been solved. According to this point of view, there was no need for the government to do more for black people because black and white were now equal. When placed in the context of 2008, Wright appeared to be an atavistic caricature of an angry black leader, a leader out of step with the supposedly "postracial" sensibilities of the time, and a man willfully ignorant of America's racial progress. If anyone was guilty of anything, it was Wright's critics for being ignorant of America's racial history and its continued legacy. We believe that this gives added weight to Gore Vidal's quip that we live "permanently in the United States of Amnesia. We learn nothing because we remember nothing."[97] Jeremiah Wright, and the members of Trinity United Church of Christ, do remember.

The Limits of Wright's Afrocentric Worldview

Reverend Jeremiah Wright is not, as some of his critics have claimed, "crazy."[98] If anything, Wright demonstrated that he is too outspoken and too identifiably black in a society that increasingly claims to be "postracial." Having said that, we also note that his understanding of the black past, and world history generally, is informed in part by Afrocentric nationalism.[99] Afrocentrists claim that Africa (by which they mean Egypt), and not ancient Greece, was the progenitor of Western culture. Such Afrocentric views have become part of a vernacular form of black nationalism.[100] Wright uses Afrocentrism in a number of his sermons.[101] For example, in a collection of his sermons entitled *Africans Who Shaped Our Faith*, Wright claims that "evidence exists within and outside the Bible to support the notion that the people of Israel, and the people of most of the empires and kingdoms that surrounded them at that time were of African descent!"[102] This is an odd assertion; it makes as much sense as the claim of Houston Stewart Chamberlain, the late nineteenth- and early twentieth-century racist, that Jesus was an Aryan.

Afrocentrism is essentially Eurocentrism dressed up in blackface. Afrocentrism attempts to invert the Romantic racialism of nineteenth-century Euro-Americans—a body of thought that maintained that blacks were naturally spiritual, among other things—by replacing it with an African chronicle of origins.[103] Wright and other black ministers who subscribe to Afrocentrism believe that Afrocentric views must form a part of their ministry to the poor and oppressed. Thus, Afrocentrism operates as a kind of revitalization movement that aims to "remove Europe as the center of black sacred life and replace it with Africa."[104] In other words, Afrocentrism constitutes a form of "mind cure" that strives to raise black self-esteem.

Attempting to elevate black self-esteem is not a new idea in black religious history. The idea that God is black is, as noted, an old one in black Christianity. If there was a need for black people to be proud and confident in the nineteenth century, that need still exists today. The problem with Wright's Afrocentric take on this black religious tradition, however, is that his Afrocentrism devolves into the very thing that his ministry has attempted to overcome: racial essentialism. Culturally, when placed in the context of world and American racial history, Afrocentrism displays the same the kind of racial arrogance that black people have criticized whites for exhibiting for generations. In the final analysis, Afrocentrism, like a number of other alternative histories, is a self-esteem project intended to recuperate a past that never was. This is something that Barack Obama recognized when he wrote that black nationalist schemes of this nature constitute "a message that ignores causality or fault, a message outside history, without a script or plot that might insist on progression."[105]

In Wright's sermons, American blacks are referred to as "Africans," something that black leaders from Frederick Douglass to Martin Luther King Jr. insisted they were not. Black people in the United States are a people of African descent, not Africans. The people Wright calls "Africans"—people who shared an African identity—did not exist in the fifteenth century, when the Atlantic slave trade began forcibly bringing West Africans to the Americas. The idea of an African identity is actually a European invention of the nineteenth century.[106] No black person arriving in the North American colonies in the seventeenth century thought of herself or himself as African. Therefore, underlying

Wright's use of the word "African" is the assumption that the history of blacks in the United States has unfolded in a continuous linear fashion, something that makes Wright a historical continuitarian. Such a view of history fails to recognize that black Americans are a new people who have mixed biologically and culturally with people from other races and ethnicities. Black Americans are not, as Afrocentrists might claim, the descendents of ancient Egyptians living in an American exile.

The history of black Americans does not fit into the synchronic paradigm of Afrocentrism. Black American history is a diachronic experience marked by enslavement, the Middle Passage, the seasoning of slaves, and their ultimate arrival in the New World, where they were forced to work alongside strangers from different parts of West Africa. Each of these steps constituted a different and distinct historical moment for the black people who became identified as Africans in North America. The image of Africa as a homogenous (and universally prosperous) black space before the arrival of Europeans is simply wishful thinking. The African continent was a diverse and dynamic place, not the site of an "unproblematic unified black identity, unfissured by differences and immune to the determinants of" time, place, and country.[107] Thus, Afrocentrism simplifies the complicated history of black people in both Africa and America.

Black America's history is a unique story that began with the largest forced migration of people in the history of the world. There would be no black people in either the Northern or Southern Hemispheres of the Americas today had Africans not sold millions of people of African descent to Europeans.[108] This is a complicated historical narrative that is not adequately addressed by Afrocentric history. If Africans were as spiritual and antimaterialistic as the Afrocentrists claim, why did Africans participate in, and seek to profit from, the Atlantic slave trade? Wright does not address such difficult topics; instead, he, like other Afrocentrists, focuses on the issues of self-esteem and identity. In his sermon "Faith in a Foreign Land," Wright incorporates the Babylonian captivity of the Jews into his Afrocentrism to explicate the problem of African cultural loss among black Americans. According to Wright:

> The African exiles who came to North America also were expected to learn the culture of their empire—"Babylon." African Americans have forgotten what their African forebears had created—the oral traditions and the written traditions. In fact, the "Babylonian" curriculum doesn't include any African authors. . . . These exiles became schooled in Babylonian literature, from *Beowulf* to Virginia Woolf, and their heritage was wickedly wiped away from the tissues of their memory banks. . . . Children of these African exiles . . . do not know a thing about one of their writers, never wrote what could be called serious classical literature. Their heritage has been taken away from them.[109]

Interestingly, Wright is here dependent on a European model of immigration and cultural transmission for his understanding of the African past and the slave trade. What Wright views as the imposition of Euro-American culture on blacks was a much more complicated story. Drawing analogies between the Jews in Babylon and blacks in America is thus inspiring but limited in its explanatory power. For example, when Wright uses the case of Queen Esther to explicate the destructive effects of assimilation, Wright claims that Esther "out-Babylonians the Babylonians. Assimilation is like that. It slowly kills you. You don't even realize what is happening to you, because when you assimilate you forget who you are. As a matter of fact, sin and assimilation are just alike."[110] Wright's final assertion is both bad religion and poor history. As Shulamit Volkov has observed in another context, assimilation "is shaded by thick ideological dust" that makes it a "complex and dialectical" process.[111] For Wright, however, assimilation is an epithet, and using assimilation in this way makes it possible for him to say that some black people are not authentically black because they have lost their Africanity. If Wright is trying to advance the idea that there was, and is, an authentic black self, he is grossly oversimplifying black history in the United States. There is no such thing as a culturally or empirically authentic history, only that which is defined as authentic. In other words, the totalitarianism of Afrocentrism works against the dynamic and contested ways in which historical narratives are constructed.

Wright's "Africans" were neither immigrants nor exiles in the New World. Blacks did not choose to come to work in the Caribbean or in North and South America. This distinguishes black America's historical experience from that of the Chinese, Germans, Irish, Japanese, or Italians in the United States. In other words, the process of cultural transmission that kept segments of European culture alive in America was not possible for many of the slaves whom Wright calls African. The letters, for example, that sustained European and Asian immigrants in America were not a part of the cultural formation of Africans in the Americas as they became Afro-Americans. Even the history that created for these Africans a sense of identity was not written, but transmitted in oral form. With time, the memories of an African past became part of hybrid Afro-American cultures, or simply died. But there is an even more egregious assumption embedded in Wright's Afrocentrism: he presents human cultures as static and unchanging. The black people who came to the American mainland after the seventeenth century could not afford to remain "African." The worlds they had come from were, if not destroyed, at least transformed by the slave trade. African culture became a distant memory for many, and survival in the American colonies required coming to grips with colonial culture and language. As a result, the maintenance of a sense of Africanity became increasingly tenuous, something that was especially true after the abolition of the international slave trade in 1808 cut off Afro-Americans from African-born slaves who could transmit African cultures and languages. Had black society in North America been replenished by new waves of slaves from Africa, black American culture in the United States might today resemble those Afro-American cultures created in Cuba, Haiti, or Brazil. Such historical insights are absent from Wright's Afrocentric views.

The transformation of black culture was not a holocaust, as some Afrocentrists claim. Just what the relevance of an African culture was and is for black people living in a Euro-Atlantic country is not entirely clear. The Afrocentrists refuse to admit, for instance, that it was important for black people to learn English in the seventeenth and eighteenth centuries. Such acculturation was an important step if black people hoped to contest the white supremacy that coalesced after the American Revolution. It was a good thing, therefore, that former slaves like Phillis Wheatley and Jupiter Hammon wrote poems and essays that counteracted the idea that black people were unthinking brutes. These two brilliantly gifted African American writers laid the groundwork for the slave narratives of Harriet Jacobs and Frederick Douglass, among others, whose written work contested the idea that blacks were incapable of learning or that slavery had broken black people. These slave narratives are an important source for understanding what black people thought about bondage.[112] Reverend Wright is not completely ignorant of the lessons contained in the American past. If white Americans give voice to a dubious understanding of black history (and American history generally), the same can be said of Afrocentrists.

Conclusion

We could continue this critique of Wright's Afrocentrism, but that would not be productive. What is unfortunate is that the work of this fine preacher has been sullied by his dissemination of Afrocentrism and by his political demonization in the white media. Wright has to know that, on some level, the problems of black people in America are not cultural—as Afrocentrism implies—but economically, socially, and politically structural issues that Afrocentrism fails to address. No amount of preaching about a glorious black past and the loss of Africanity can change the conditions of life for the black urban poor. Obama knows this, and as we demonstrate in the next chapter, other prominent black leaders over the past thirty years have recognized that what black people truly need is a useable present that corrects the continuing impact of history's ills. At some level, Wright himself recognizes this need, as his inspiring sermon "The Audacity to Hope" made clear when he urged black people to "hope when the love of God [was] not plainly evident."[113] This is the Reverend Jeremiah Wright at his best.

It is important to remember that the fact that Barack Obama attended Wright's church for twenty years does not mean he agrees with everything his preacher said. As a teenager, one of us (Clarence E. Walker) attended a storefront Baptist church in which the minister preached that evolution was a lie, that the Baptist Church was the first church in the world because of John the Baptist, and that man could not travel to the moon. Neither Walker nor his friends accepted these statements of clerical wisdom. In other words, black people do not blindly follow their ministers; rather, they attend church services, just as white Americans do, for a variety of reasons. Fellowship, music, preaching, and seeing and being seen all motivate African Americans to be part of a church community. Reverend Wright attracted some eight thousand worshippers to the Trinity community not for his preaching alone, but for the sense of community that Trinity United Church of Christ provided.

Wright, as we have tried to show, is part of a grand tradition of black churchmen. Wright's observation after 9/11 that the "chickens are coming home to roost" was not impolitic, but a blunt assessment of the historical impact of American foreign policy. It is ironic, if not risible, that it took the manufactured scandal surrounding Wright's sermons, and his twenty-year friendship with President Obama, to remind the cour Obama is not "postracial": he is black, and he self-iden such. To deny this identity to Obama is to attempt to re[illegible] whiteness as normative under the guise of "postracialism." That Obama, like Wright, has chosen to self-identify as black is one of the most basic human rights that he can exercise, to which we say, Amen.

"I Don't Want People to Pretend I'm Not Black"

Barack Obama and America's Racial History

The media controversy surrounding Barack Obama's relationship with Reverend Wright demonstrated how racial issues continue to divide Americans. As we noted in the preceding chapter, Obama was a member of a black church whose minister espoused racial pride and self-help, and delivered sermons that offered an unflinching critique of contemporary racial injustices. In a society that lays claim to being "postracial," black ministers like Wright present a challenge to the "color-blind" whitewashing of American society. Obama's membership in Trinity United Church of Christ served to emphasize his "blackness" and poses a serious challenge to those who portray him as a poster child for "postracialism." For all the media discussion of how Obama transcends historical racial boundaries, Obama has publicly identified himself as a black American. While conscious of the complexities of contemporary race relations, Obama confounds both liberal adherents to "postracialism" and conservatives who espouse "color blindness" when he states: "I don't want people to pretend I'm not black."[1]

Obama's mixed-race parentage, his self-identification as a black man, and his two-decade-long membership in a black church that espouses racial pride confront all Americans with the complexities and contradictions of the United States’ racial history. Obama’s “A More Perfect Union” speech, delivered in Philadelphia on March 18, 2008, addressed this difficult history and attempted to answer any electoral concerns about his relationship with Reverend Wright. (See p. 105 for the text of this speech.) As a political statement, Obama’s speech did two things: it echoed the sense of racial pride that Wright emphasized at Trinity, and it highlighted the points related to contemporary racial issues on which Obama and Wright disagree.[2] This speech, like Obama’s previous writings and speeches, attempted to convey the subtleties that he sees in America’s racial history. While the United States has a past stained by “the original sin of slavery,” it also has a history in which the optimistic words of the Founding Fathers echo through the ages: “We the people, in order to form a more perfect union.”[3] In this chapter, we address the complex and often contradictory nature of American racial history that Obama identified in his “A More Perfect Union” speech. We analyze how Obama has become an important part of the history of mixed-race people in North America and situate his personal narrative within the larger history of race mixing in the United States. We then turn our attention to the role of black people in American politics and consider the historical significance of Obama’s rise to the presidency of the United States. As we demonstrate, race, mixed-race identity, religious affiliation, and national politics have a long, complex, and interconnected history that exposes the inadequacies of terms like “postracial” and “color blindness.”

A Brief History of Mixed-Race People in the United States

In 2005, data from the United States Census Bureau revealed that approximately 3 percent of the American population self-identified as mixed-race.[4] While census figures can hide as much as they reveal (obscuring, for example, regional variations in interracial marriage patterns), it is telling that a significant majority of Americans, approximately 75.1 percent, continue to categorize themselves with a single racial group, the Census category of "white."[5] In the current demographic context, Obama identifies himself with the mere 3 percent of the population whom the Census Bureau classifies as "mixed-race," a designation that undermines the neat single-race categories used by the U.S. federal government. Obama also represents a utopian racial vision of the United States, a self-consciously mixed-race vision of the American republic that confounds the historical quest for a "white" republic as outlined in the naturalization law of 1790, which stated that only "free white persons" could become citizens of the United States.[6]

That a majority of Americans self-identify with a single racial group helps us understand why some voters remained suspicious of Obama during 2007–8. Suspicion of mixed-race Americans is deeply embedded in the United States' racial history, dating back to the colonial foundations of the republic. Obama's skill as a politician, his brilliant speechmaking, and the Republican Party's inability to articulate a coherent set of strategies for tackling the social and economic problems that face ordinary Americans contributed to his election victory. Obama's victory, however, did not eliminate the historical legacy of race, racism, and race mixing in America; rather, his candidacy and ultimate triumph highlight the contested meanings that Americans attach to racial identities. Obama's complex personal narrative helped to refocus American attention on the racial aspects of American identity, religion, and patriotism. For example, when journalists asked Sarah Palin, the Republican Party's vice-presidential nominee, about Obama's relationship with Reverend Jeremiah Wright, Palin responded: "I don't know why that association isn't discussed more."[7] Suspicions about a black—and particularly a mixed-race—political candidate's "radical" and allegedly unpatriotic associations with religious and political leaders are not new to American politics, society, and culture, and continue to resonate with small sections of the voting public.

Obama has become an important part of the history of mixed-race people in the United States. This history dates back to the seventeenth-century colonies of northeastern America. Spanish, Dutch, French, and English settlers intermingled sexually and socially with each other, and with Native Americans and African slaves, just as indigenous Americans amalgamated with Africans and Europeans. Racial mixture throughout the Americas was thus complex and fraught with the inequalities of sociopolitical power that accompanied European colonialism in the seventeenth century and beyond.[8] The historian Joel Williamson argues that, in the seventeenth and early eighteenth centuries, lawmakers in colonies such as Virginia, Maryland, and Pennsylvania saw mixed-race people as dangerous and destabilizing elements in the colonial population.[9] To colonial leaders, a mixed-race population represented the fulfillment of the worst fears of Britain's Enlightenment philosophers. According to the historian Andrew Fitzmaurice, a number of "Enlightenment thinkers" opposed colonialism "on the basis that humanity is constituted through its *mores* and that the *mores* of different people are incommensurable."[10] In colonial North America, a growing anxiety about the future place of racially mixed people prompted legislatures to act decisively in an attempt to limit the growth of mixed-race populations.[11] Colonial elites passed laws that prohibited interracial marriage and that defined mixed-race children, many of whom were the offspring of enslaved women and white overseers or slave masters, according to the condition of the mother—that is, black and enslaved. Such laws were a reminder of how even fair-skinned children born to African American women had their station in society—particularly southern slave society—fixed by sociolegal convention over the course of the eighteenth century. Colonial laws therefore laid the foundation for the American republic's racial logic of hypodescent, in which an individual with even "one drop" of black blood was designated as black rather than as white or mixed-race.[12]

The growth and westward expansion of racial slavery during the early republic and antebellum era fostered the social separation of white from black Americans, no matter how fair-skinned members of the latter group may have been. In his March 2008 "A More Perfect Union" speech, Obama referred to slavery as "this nation's original sin."[13] As Obama recognized, slavery and its attendant racial issues (such as the growth of mixed-race populations) divided the Founding Fathers in their efforts to create "a more perfect union."[14] In fact, the political compromises made over the issue of slavery during the late eighteenth and early nineteenth centuries meant that the union developed in a decidedly imperfect fashion. Slavery thus structured American society along racial lines and fostered a sectional political divide that culminated in bloody internecine warfare. The Civil War (1861–65), which eventually led to the abolition of slavery with the enactment of the Thirteenth Amendment (1865), undermined the socioeconomic and legal basis for the white supremacist social order that racial slavery buttressed in large portions of the United States, and placed the republic on the path to attaining what black Americans felt was the ideal of "a more perfect union."

In much of the postbellum South, however, whites felt that the abolition of slavery and the enfranchisement of African American men had the potential to produce the unnatural condition of "nigger rule."[15] The "one-drop rule," which became particularly important in the South, was instrumental in restoring to the South an idealized antebellum racial order. Where slavery once stood as a visible sign of white supremacy, the articulation of the "one-drop rule" in America's legal system and popular culture served to restructure late nineteenth-century American society along biological lines. A number of prominent political leaders attempted to increase their political power by appealing to the racial prejudices to which the "one-drop rule" pandered.

In 1868, for example, the Democratic Party nominee for president, Horatio Seymour, ran on the slogan "This is a white man's country: Let white men rule." Seymour narrowly lost the 1868 presidential election to the Civil War hero Ulysses S. Grant.[16] By the late 1880s and early 1890s, however, the slogan that defined Seymour's failed presidential campaign was increasingly written into state laws and Supreme Court decisions.[17] As the legal scholar Ariela Gross argues, the "one-drop rule" became part of a "post–Civil War effort to implement Jim Crow legislation."[18]

The "one-drop rule" provided the "scientific," and therefore objective, logic necessary to outlaw interracial marriage and pass laws in a number of southern and western states that segregationist politicians believed would result in "a more perfect union." The segregation laws that became synonymous with the Jim Crow South confined African Americans to low-paying occupations, geographically segregated black people away from white neighborhoods in substandard housing, and, critically, emphasized membership in a single racial group on the basis of the "one-drop rule."[19] In other words, the South's broad definition of "blackness" structured social life and rationalized the institutionalization of racism in large sections of the United States.[20] In postbellum Louisiana, for example, a state with a long history of race mixing, the Bureau of Vital Statistics used the practice of "race flagging" to prevent parents who looked white, but had "black" blood, from applying for a birth certificate that designated their child as white. The practice of "race flagging" aimed to prevent the growth of the "mulatto" population. As the architects of the Jim Crow South saw the issue of race mixing, the existence of mixed-race children "was a profound indictment of the biracial Southern system."[21]

During the late nineteenth and early twentieth centuries, with evolutionary and social Darwinian theories influencing American racial perceptions and social practices, the presence of a "mulatto" population was seen by some Americans as a threat to the purity of white blood and civilization. White Americans from different class and religious backgrounds read, discussed, and worried about the "rising tide of color."[22] People of Asian, African, and Middle Eastern descent were assumed to present an evolutionary challenge to the "white man's" republic and a threat, not to the "ideal of equal citizenship under the law," as Obama has repeatedly stated, but to the ideal of equal citizenship among whites. Scholars refer to this racialized definition of citizenship as "herrenvolk democracy," a concept that maintains legal equality for whites only.[23] In the early twentieth century, the eugenicist Lothrop Stoddard wrote about the potentially "dysgenic" effects that social and sexual intermixture between whites and blacks would have on American democracy: "This insidious disease [of race mixing], with its twin symptoms of extirpation of superior strains and the multiplication of inferiors, has ravaged humanity like a consuming fire, reducing the proudest societies to charred and squalid ruin."[24]

Stoddard's work articulated the early twentieth-century fear that the white races in America were under siege from inferior colored races.[25] Fueling these fears was a growing number of disturbing reports that suggested African Americans were "passing" as white and, even more terrifying, marrying and copulating with unsuspecting white men and women. The answer to such racial deception was the racial identification of individuals by phenotypal (or physical) differences, and genotypal (that is, genetic) distinctions. In other words, because race could not always be discerned from skin color and physiognomic characteristics, racial identity was now increasingly linked to microscopic portions of human blood—just "one drop" of "black" blood was enough to make one a "Negro." As one historian argues: "Southerners came to fear hidden blackness, the blackness within seeming whiteness. They began to look with great suspicion upon mulattoes who looked white, white people who behaved as blacks, and a whole congeries of aliens insidious in their midst who would destroy their happily whole moral universe."[26]

Barack Obama has written and spoken about the history of race mixing in America. His reflections on the subject echo the sense of shame and uncertainty that has for generations gripped mixed-race people. Obama, for example, wrote in *Dreams from My Father* about the suspicious looks that his mixed-race appearance has elicited from white people. Like mixed-race Americans in generations before him, Obama grew to understand that these quizzical glances betrayed the viewer's sense that he, a mixed-race American male, was in some way illegitimate, quite possibly angry, and at the end of the day, little more than a confused "Negro"—a "tragic mulatto"—who wanted to be white. Obama's rise to the presidency may ultimately help to eliminate such sentiments, but his writings and speeches do reflect his hard-won understanding that mixed-race people have long been considered problematic elements in the creation of "a more perfect union."

Obama's autobiographical reflections on his "blackness" also remind readers of the sense of uncertainty that black Americans have often felt in a nation defined by its white hegemonic culture. Obama's writings on this subject are in the self-reflective tradition that is a trademark of black literature. Take, for example, Richard Wright's discussion of "blackness" in his landmark novel *Native Son* (1940). In that work, Wright describes through the novel's protagonist, Bigger Thomas, how white stares make African American people feel their "blackness." Wright writes that Bigger was made to "feel his black skin" when Mary, the white daughter of his employer, and Jan, her white male friend, were "just standing there looking at him, one holding his hand and the other smiling. He felt that he had no physical existence at all right then; he was something he hated, the badge of shame which he knew was attached to a black skin."[27]

Obama has described how, in post–civil rights movement America, he was able to overcome the sense of "shame" that Wright and other African American authors describe. Obama's "A More Perfect Union" speech, for example, reflected his unapologetic identification as a unique product of American racial mixing:

> I am the son of a black man from Kenya and a white woman from Kansas. I was raised with the help of a white grandfather who survived a Depression to serve in Patton's Army during World War II and a white grandmother who worked on a bomber assembly line at Fort Leavenworth while he was overseas. I've gone to some of the best schools in America and lived in one of the world's poorest nations. I am married to a black American who carries within her the blood of slaves and slaveowners—an inheritance we pass on to our two precious daughters. I have brothers, sisters, nieces, nephews, uncles and cousins, of every race and every hue, scattered across three continents, and for as long as I live, I will never forget that in no other country on Earth is my story even possible.[28]

Here, as in his books and speeches, Obama repeated his family narrative in a way that neutralized any suspicions that he might be "angry" about slavery and Jim Crow, and that demystified his statistically atypical parentage and upbringing. Obama, like millions of Americans, is the son of an immigrant. However, while Obama's family narrative has been presented to fit into the master narrative of immigration and assimilation, Obama's father was no ordinary African immigrant: he was one of the few Africans to migrate to the United States freely, and he became better educated than most Americans, white or black. At the same time, Obama has had to contend with the fact that his father was both African and Muslim, something Americans might find disconcerting. President Obama has handled these issues by focusing, as he did in his inaugural speech, on how his father grew up in a "small village," just as millions of Americans grow up and start families in the small towns that make up the American heartland. In this rhetorical balancing act, Obama has attempted to make mundane, safe, and commonplace what is truly a remarkable family story. At times during the 2008 presidential campaign, Obama was forced to tread carefully to maintain this delicate balancing act.[29]

While Obama’s personal narrative is far from the typical family narrative of most Americans, it is also not as foreign as some Americans might imagine or as Census Bureau statistics might lead us to believe. We have already sketched the brief history of race mixing in North America, and Obama’s own writings reflect an understanding of this history.[30] For example, Obama demonstrated his understanding of the power of words to define a people when, in *Dreams from My Father,* he wrote that the word “miscegenation,” the nineteenth- and twentieth-century term used to describe race mixing, is “humpbacked, ugly, [and] portending a monstrous outcome.”[31] The reason Obama has elicited such optimism in so many Americans is that he has confronted this history and seems to offer the nation an opportunity to move beyond its “monstrous” past.

Obama’s life story has been used to undermine America’s racist history and replace it with a multiracial narrative of immigrants coming together and uniting around a core of democratic ideals. This powerful narrative is not a reflection of Obama’s “postracial” vision of American democracy, as some of his supporters might wish, but of his liberal worldview.[32] While Obama’s liberal assimilationist views may not seem particularly radical in a twenty-first-century “postracial” context, placed against the history of the past century, Obama’s determination to have Americans recommit to the creation of “a more perfect union” is a progressive, if not radical, position that does not seek to whitewash black identity with conservative theories of “color blindness” and sophomoric notions of “postracialism.”

The embrace of the concepts of “color blindness” and “postracialism” threaten to breed in American culture a dangerous level of historical amnesia. Such forgetting is dangerous to American democracy not simply because it raises fears about repeating history’s mistakes, but because generations of Americans see racism as an aberration of the past and fail to understand just how central racism has been to American democracy. There are many ways that one can come to an appreciation of this, but the most accessible medium is popular culture. In the early twentieth century, for example, hugely successful novels like Thomas Dixon's *The Clansman* (1905) portrayed white America's fear of political equality with blacks in the most profound way possible: through overly sexualized imagery of black men and women. Black men were of particular concern to authors like Dixon, who portrayed African American men as unscrupulous in their political ambition, savage in their manners, and sexually insatiable. In *The Clansman*, the prototypical "Negro" beast was Gus, who had "thick cracked lips," a "huge jaw," and "coarse bestiality."[33] Typical of the white women in Dixon's story was Marian Lenoir, "a sixteen-year-old beauty rapidly ripening into ideal womanhood," a picture of "grace and symmetry . . . a living flower."[34] The delicate beauty of Lenoir, not unlike the South before "Negro rule," appeared to millions of southerners to have been laid prostrate, ready for savage, well-endowed black men to sate their lust.[35]

D. W. Griffith brought these once widely held fears to life in his classic 1915 film *Birth of a Nation*.[36] Griffith's film adaptation of Dixon's *The Clansman* was an explicitly racist narrative of Reconstruction in the American South. His movie focused on characters such as Silas Lynch, a power-hungry, sex-crazed "mulatto" politician. Lynch was the embodiment of "black villainy" and lawlessness, a stark contrast to the "white innocence" of white female characters such as Elsie Stoneman (played by Lillian Gish), the daughter of a prominent abolitionist.[37] Griffith's portrayal of white women as innocent, vulnerable, and subject to defilement by power-hungry black "bucks" was a metonym for the emasculated South.[38] The film scholar Donald Bogle argues that what white southerners truly feared, and what Griffith portrayed, was the "big, baadddd niggers, oversexed and savage, violent and frenzied as they lust for white flesh."[39]

While Obama did not attract the same degree of racial caricaturing during his 2008 bid for the White House, the anxiety he caused some white Americans was in some ways as acute as that expressed in the fictional rendering of Silas Lynch in the early twentieth century. Where Lynch was corrupt, power-hungry, and lusted after the flesh of a white woman, Obama, according to his critics, was corrupt and possessed of an unscrupulous determination to rule not simply a state, but the entire nation. These contemporary anxieties were expressed during the 2008 presidential campaign.[40] One blogger, for example, claimed in July 2008 that Obama "has a very corrupt past history that the media has refused to discuss. seems he has directed alot of tax dollars to his own special interest groups that has paid off very well for him."[41] In the early twentieth century, a number of white Americans worried about the political implications of the so-called "mulatto advantage," the belief that mixed-race African Americans possessed economic and political advantages over darker-skinned people.[42] The sociologist Earnest S. Cox articulated a more anxious version of the "mulatto advantage" in American politics, arguing that most African American politicians were "mongrels who have the ear of the white man."[43] Mercifully, mainstream media and academic writing no longer purvey such crude racism; however, as the comments of the blogger quoted above suggest, some in the American electorate continue to harbor stereotypes of mixed-race politicians like Obama having the power to cast magical spells over the American media and to co-opt "special interest groups" to support their candidacy.

Historically constructed perceptions of corrupt black politicians and duplicitous mixed-race Americans dogged Obama at various points during his 2008 presidential campaign. One Internet blogger, for instance, accused Obama of being a deceptive politician in terms reminiscent of the caricatured portrait of Silas Lynch in *Birth of a Nation:* "Obama has not produced a valid birth certificate, Obama is a cunning lying serpent narcissist."[44] Since World War II, racialized comments of this nature have come under periodic scrutiny by producers of American popular culture. Starting with films like Louis de Rochemont's *Lost Boundaries* (1949) and Elia Kazan's *Pinky* (1949), and culminating more recently with Spike Lee's *Bamboozled* (2000), filmmakers have produced movies that reflect changes in American racial attitudes, and that force American audiences to confront issues like interracial sex and marriage, multiracial identity, and "passing."[45] In *Lost Boundaries,* for example, de Rochemont portrays the phenotypically white Dr. Scott Carter, a beloved member of a small New England community. Carter is exposed as a "Negro" after his patriotism gets the better of him and he enlists in the United States Navy. A routine examination of medical and birth records reveals, to the horror of local residents, the existence of "Negro blood" in Carter's veins. Only after an emotional sermon by the community's white minister are the townspeople persuaded to overlook Carter's biological heritage and "extend their hands again to their friends."[46]

In its call for racial tolerance, de Rochemont's "problem film" was ahead of public sentiment. In fact, films like *Lost Boundaries* can in a small way be seen as a popular culture response to Gunnar Myrdal's two-volume study of America's "Negro problem." In *An American Dilemma* (1944), Myrdal, a Swedish lawyer who had been commissioned by the Carnegie Corporation to study race relations in the United States, found that no issue pressed more heavily on American anxieties than race mixing and light-skinned African Americans "passing" as white. According to Myrdal, concerns about passing rested on the assumption that mixed-race people feel a sense of rootlessness.[47] Early twentieth-century scholars like Myrdal claimed that it was a sense of rootlessness that drove "mulattoes" to enter politics in a bid to feel a degree of communal connectedness. The problem, however, was that "mulatto" leaders were accused by whites of increasing racial tensions. The sociologist Grove Samuel Dow incorporated these perceptions into his 1920 study *Society and Its Problems*, asserting that "it is no wonder that it is the mulatto who has been a factor in race friction. Whereas the bulk of the black Negroes accepted their position of inferiority, the mulatto has been less willing to do so."[48] Did those Americans who expressed the most incendiary views about Obama's bid for the White House share a modern version of Dow's analysis? When Georgia Republican representative Lynn Westmoreland called Obama "uppity," we received a reminder that some Americans continue to feel uncomfortable with black elected officials.[49]

The election results on November 4, 2008, suggest that Westmoreland's views are not as widespread as they once were. This may account for the American public's captivation with Obama's life story, something that would not have been possible a generation ago. Indeed, the bitter and often violent struggles of the civil rights movement during the 1950s and 1960s, civil rights laws, and the 1967 *Loving* decision in the U.S. Supreme Court (which made it legal for black and white couples to marry) made it possible for an American like Obama to run for and win the highest elective office in the land. Obama's victory indicated that profound racial changes have occurred in the United States over the last half century. And yet, despite these advances, it is telling that Obama, like so many other mixed-race Americans, continues to speak publicly about his racial struggles and the quest for a sense of community. This is because interracial sexuality and racial identity are issues that still cause much public discomfort. In 2004, for example, then Philadelphia Eagles football star Terrell Owens was embroiled in controversy after he appeared in a National Football League television commercial. Owens was featured alongside the white actress Nicollette Sheridan, who dropped the towel she was wearing, suggesting that she was standing naked in front of the black football star. The commercial caused outrage among many viewers, prompting the University of Philadelphia's Michael Eric Dyson to comment that the "notion of a big, black buck with a vulnerable, dainty white female still stirs controversy in the minds of so many people."[50] Dyson's analysis of the NFL advertisement suggests that interracial sex and mixed-race identities remain hot-button issues in American racial discourse.

The Memoir of a Mixed-Race American

Barack Obama's memoir *Dreams from My Father* (1995) attempts to take on the historically freighted topic of interracial marriage and mixed-race identity, and transform his personal narrative into a positive statement about a multiracial republic. While Obama strives to project optimism in the political arena, his memoir reflects a complex understanding of race, of late twentieth-century anxieties about mixed-race people, and of the historical changes in American society since the 1960s. While millions of Americans have become enthralled by Obama's story, some Americans, both black and white, have greeted Obama's political rise with quizzical and often polemical statements about his race and political views. In the post–civil rights movement, post–Reagan revolution, "postracial" America, just how exactly are people like Obama meant to understand American society? How are Americans meant to understand people like Obama? Where do mixed-race people fit in contemporary society? Do they have to fit anywhere? Charles Barkley, an African American and former star in the National Basketball League, gave voice to these questions and the uncertainty of the answers that they often produce when he claimed in his memoir, *Who's Afraid of a Large Black Man?* (2005), that Obama is "hard to peg."[51]

During the 2008 presidential election, some Americans were as confounded as Barkley in their attempts to "peg" Obama. According to news reports during 2008, millions reverted to well-worn racial stereotyping when referring to Obama. For example, at a campaign rally for Sarah Palin in October 2008, television news cameras spotted an elderly white man carrying a toy monkey with an Obama sticker attached to its forehead. The gentleman referred to the monkey as "Hussein."[52] American celebrities were not immune from engaging in similarly crude racializations of Obama. Harkening back to an era when white Americans believed that "passing" was a symptom of black Americans pretending to be something (and someone) they were not, the country music singer Toby Keith claimed that Obama acted white in an effort to win white voters. Appearing with the conservative radio and television personality Glenn Beck, Keith insisted, "I think the black people would say he [Obama] don't talk, act or carry himself as a black person."[53]

Obama is all too aware of these racial perceptions. In *Dreams from My Father*, he offers his perspective on what was once known as the "tragic mulatto" complex. He insists that "miscegenation"—a neologism coined by a Democratic Party propagandist named David Croly in 1864 to denote interracial sexual mixing between black and white people and their mixed-race offspring—was an "ugly" word "portending a monstrous outcome: like *antebellum* or *octoroon*, it evokes images of another era, a distant world of horsewhips and flames, dead magnolias and crumbling porticos."[54] With words reminiscent of W. E. B. Du Bois's famous "double consciousness, this sense of always looking at one's self through the eyes of others," Obama continued to describe his personal exploration of racial identity by placing himself in the historical context of the confused, troubled, or artful "tragic mulatto" of American literature.[55] He did this, in part, by recounting the reactions he has encountered after people learn of his mixed-race parentage: "I see the split-second adjustments they have to make, the searching of my eyes for some telltale sign. They no longer know who I am. Privately, they guess at my troubled heart, I suppose—the mixed blood, the divided soul, the ghostly image of the tragic mulatto trapped between two worlds."[56]

In public statements on the issue of racial identity since 2004, Obama attempted to mediate, particularly for white audiences, the harsh racial reality contained in such statements.

Speaking on NPR's *All Things Considered* in 2004, Obama claimed that the "African American community is, by definition, a hybrid culture. We draw on these different elements . . . as I've grown up in the United States, I have been identified as an African American. I'm comfortable with that identification. I'm rooted in that culture and draw inspiration from that tradition."[57] Obama was here attempting to allay public—and perhaps his own—fears that he embodied a modern version of the duplicitous and "uppity" fictional character Silas Lynch, or that he was acting white, and therefore was a "tragic mulatto" pretending to be somebody he was not. While the crude language used to describe the "mulatto" has faded from popular consciousness, suspicions about power-hungry "mulatto" politicians and black concerns that the rising mixed-race political star will turn out to be an "Uncle Tom" (and turn his back on the African American community) continue to be expressed in American cultural discourse.[58]

Obama has become all too aware of these perceptions. In his "A More Perfect Union" speech, he observed how "some commentators have deemed me either 'too black' or "not black enough.'"[59] Obama's life story is more than a political football; it is a profound contribution to a growing literature written by and about mixed-race Americans. This literature emphasizes America's multiracial diversity and has played a significant role in eroding the offensive "tragic mulatto" imagery in American popular culture. Some of the most prominent examples of this burgeoning genre include a memoir by the journalist Edward Ball, who discovered an interracial family history that reached back into the dark recesses of slavery in the American South. Others, such as Shirlee Taylor Haizlip, state boldly, but not incorrectly, "that there are no 'real white Americans.'"[60] And Rebecca Walker, the daughter of the African American writer Alice Walker and the Jewish civil rights attorney Mel Leventhal, along with Essie Mae Washington-Williams, the mixed-race "love child" of the arch-segregationist Strom Thurmond, give voice to a history in which race and sexuality intersect in very color-conscious ways to produce a multiracial human tapestry.[61]

Obama's *Dreams from My Father* has added significantly to this genre of autobiographical writing. Far from telling the story of an America where "everybody was the same," *Dreams from My Father* is a candid exploration of mixed-race black identity in late twentieth-century America. Obama's story weaves together the hardworking ethos of his white Kansas family and the immigrant optimism that he inherited from his largely absentee Kenyan father. The story of Obama's life begins with his description of the small-town Kansas community that his grandparents and white mother, Ann, came from. Obama writes that his mother was born into a community, like so many other small towns in mid-twentieth-century Kansas, in which "fear and lack of imagination choke your dreams so that you already know on the day that you're born just where you'll die and who it is that'll bury you."[62] In this social environment, authority figures were never questioned, the Bible was literal truth, and homespun wisdom trumped the "fancy ideas" of the bookish and learned.[63]

Obama recalls that his grandmother grew up in a family that practiced "straight-backed Methodism," while his grandfather, a Baptist who looked like a "wop," won his grandmother's affections despite—or perhaps because of—the protestations of family members. Obama adds that his grandparents spent very little time thinking about blacks.[64] "Blacks," Obama states of the Midwest that his grandparents knew, "are there but not there, like Sam the piano player or Beulah the maid or Amos and Andy on the radio—shadowy, silent presences that elicit neither passion nor fear."[65] In a world in which segregation shaped American social, economic, and political norms, white people from Obama's grandparents' generation did not feel the need to invent phrases like "postrace" or "color-blind" because their racial power was generally taken for granted. Only when white identity, political power, or economic privilege was challenged did white Kansans revert to violence. This was the case in the summer of 1920, when the small town of Independence, Kansas, witnessed violent attacks and race riots that targeted African Americans. Racial outbursts of this nature punctuated the social tranquility of towns across the Midwest during the early twentieth century, and no doubt shaped the racial views of Obama's grandparents. In the 1950s, however, Obama's grandparents left the Midwest behind them and set out for a new life and new economic opportunities that would ultimately lead them to Hawaii.[66]

Obama's grandparents and mother arrived in Hawaii in 1959, the same year that the islands received the status of statehood. Hawaii was a racially diverse society, a far cry from the predominantly white world of small-town Kansas. In 1960, the United States Census Bureau, imposing the mainland's racial "division of the population into two groups, white and nonwhite," estimated that 202,230 people of the total state population of 632,772 were "white."[67] White Americans were therefore a minority in the racially diverse island chain, and it was in Hawaii that Obama's mother, Ann, met a dark-skinned Kenyan by the name of Barack Obama. Obama Sr., from a poor Muslim family in Kenya, was a student at the University of Hawaii, Manoa. Ann and Barack Sr. fell in love and married in the 1960s. The couple had a son, Barack Obama Jr., though Obama's parents separated while he was still in his infancy. The bulk of *Dreams from My Father* recounts Obama's quest to know the man whose name he shares. While his father remained "opaque" as Obama grew to manhood, his mother instilled in him a sense of right and wrong and idealism, and provided an intellectual foundation for understanding "black history."[68] Obama's homeschooling in African American history was, with the exception of a brief period when he lived with his mother and her second husband in Indonesia, received in Hawaii. Of growing up in Hawaii, Obama recalls that he was close to his white grandparents, and that he attended the elite Punahou School. In this relatively privileged context, Obama remembers, he did not arrive at a sense of racial consciousness until the age of seven or eight. As Obama remembers of his formative years, "That my father looked nothing like the people around me—that he was black as pitch, my mother white as milk—barely registered in my mind."[69] Hawaii, according to Obama's childhood memory, was a place of "racial harmony."[70]

Sunshine, surf, and elite private schools in the racial "melting pot" of Hawaii during the 1960s and 1970s was a long way from the racial tensions, race riots, gang violence, and urban poverty that characterized life for millions of blacks on the mainland.[71] Indeed, Alan Keyes, one of a handful of black Republican politicians in modern America, has gone so far as to suggest that Obama is "not really black enough."[72] Obama has acknowledged that growing up in Hawaii was a far cry from a childhood spent in the black ghettoes of Boston, New York, Chicago, or Los Angeles. In fact, Obama characterizes Hawaii as a racial utopia. He observes that Hawaii did not experience the racial violence of mainland American cities, nor did it have the antimiscegenation laws that would have made his parents' marriage illegal throughout much of the mainland South. However, Obama's racial memories of Hawaii are embellished with the idealism and innocence of childhood. "There were too many races," Obama recalls, "with power among them too diffuse, to impose the mainland's rigid caste system; and so few blacks that the most ardent segregationist could enjoy a vacation secure in the knowledge that race mixing in Hawaii had little to do with the established order back home."[73] Obama may have embellished some of his memories, but his insights nonetheless provide an important insight into his racial optimism, and begin to explain why this son of the American tropics—and not the Deep South, or Harlem, or Roxbury in Boston—is seen by many Americans as the president best equipped to lead the United States into a "postracial" future.

The African American population in nineteenth- and early twentieth-century Hawaii was tiny, reaching a mere 4,943, according to the 1960 Census (the year after Obama's grandparents arrived in Oahu).[74] Despite the small black population in Hawaii, racial attitudes toward people of African descent, and darker-skinned people generally, were not completely dissimilar from those in mainland North America.[75] For example, Miles M. Jackson has observed that late nineteenth-century Hawaiian plantation owners went against public opinion by pushing for a migration scheme that would bring black workers from the mainland.[76] According to one plantation owner: "Two Negroes can do the work of three Japanese. . . . The women will work as well as the men at about two-thirds the wages. Interest has also been awakened among housewives as to the desirability of Negroes as cooks, nurses, etc. and many think they may supplant the Japanese in household duties."[77]

As on the mainland, African Americans were envisioned as menial laborers in Hawaii's agricultural economy, a proletarian economic status reinforced by their lowly social position and political powerlessness throughout the islands. Hawaiian plantation owners did not get the large black labor force for which they had hoped. Instead, Asian and Polynesian laborers toiled under the hot tropical sun, a demographic development that may explain why discussions of race mixing in Hawaii were more open than on the mainland during the first half of the twentieth century. Obama does not explore this aspect of Hawaiian history, but an army of early twentieth-century sociologists and anthropologists did travel to the islands and conduct research on race mixing. The reports that these studies produced concluded that a "strikingly attractive" new race was emerging in "race's experiment garden" in the Pacific.[78] What made racial "hybridization" acceptable to scholars of the Hawaiian Islands was the relative absence of black people. As the historian David Hollinger observes, "Americans have mixed in certain ways and not others, and they have talked about it in certain ways and not others."[79] Intermarriage in twentieth-century Hawaii was a classic example of this selective approach to race mixing. The anthropologist E. A. Hooton, for example, noted in 1926 that intermarriages in Hawaii involving Hawaiian European and Hawaiian Chinese couples produced offspring exhibiting "hybrid vigor."[80] Nevertheless, tensions in Hawaii regarding race mixing did exist. In 1931, native Hawaiian men were alleged to have raped Thalia Massie, a white naval wife, prompting vigilante violence reminiscent of a southern lynch mob that exposed the fragility of race relations in Hawaii.[81]

Obama's autobiography does not address incidents like the Massie affair. Such omissions lend credibility to his portrayal of Hawaii as a racial utopia, and to the image that supporters of Obama have developed of the president as a racial unifier who will guide the United States into a "postracial" future. However, Obama's own narrative contains complexities that are not addressed by this politicized notion of "postracialism." In *Dreams from My Father,* for instance, Obama describes how during his teenage years he began to develop an understanding of the complexities of racial identity. At the Punahou School, Obama joined the basketball team, a decision that saw him gravitate toward a small group of black students; he also immersed himself in the classics of African American literature—from novels by Richard Wright to Malcolm X's stirring memoir.[82] During their image-conscious and sexually charged teenage years, Obama and his black friends lamented what they saw as the sexual racism of white and Asian girls in Hawaii. His African American friend "Ray," for example, complained: "These girls are A-1, USDA-certified racists. All of 'em. White girls. Asian girls—shoot, these Asians worse than the whites. Think we got a disease or something."[83]

Within African American communities, discussion of interracial sex, marriage, and mixed-race identity is often candid, and a major source of intraracial disputes. These discussions, and the politics of color within African American society, have their origins in American slavery. As such, stories of rape and coercive sexual practices in the plantation South are the starting point for many African American dialogues on race and sex. The historian Robert Toplin, for example, argues that the famous distinction between "house slaves" and "field slaves" was, in part, a product of coercive interracial sex: "Masters chose mulattoes for household duties because the 'mixed-race' was more susceptible to improvement and could handle tasks requiring higher capabilities."[84] The South's white masters nurtured these perceptions by providing specialized training for many mixed-race slaves, thereby ensuring a socioeconomic basis for a light-skinned "mulatto" elite to emerge in both ante- and postbellum America. Indeed, after the Civil War, mixed-race African Americans formed elite social clubs that based membership on the amount of "white blood" an individual possessed. "Blue-vein" clubs and "Brown Fellowship" societies sprang up throughout the United States, most refusing membership to African Americans whose skin color and physiognomy was too "Negroid."[85] A number of black churches also imposed restrictive racial demands on membership. According to one scholar: "In some churches a fine-toothed comb was hung from the front door. All persons wanting to join the church had to be able to pass the comb smoothly through their hair. If the hair was too kinky, membership was denied."[86] Such intraracial discrimination began to decline during the latter half of the twentieth century. However, questions about group and individual identity have not been entirely eliminated from African American culture. During the civil rights movement, interracial dating between black and white volunteers caused tensions among young black people. More recently, the success of African American political leaders like Obama, Adrian Fenty, and Cory Booker, all of whom appear at ease among white as well as black voters, has elicited crude characterizations from a generation of black leaders fading from the national spotlight. For example, Sharpe Jones has labeled Cory Booker a "faggot white boy," and Jesse Jackson responded to Obama's criticism of delinquent black fathers with children born out of wedlock with his infamous quip that he would like "to cut his [Obama's] nuts off" (Jackson himself was the son of unmarried parents).[87]

The emotionally fraught issue of interracial mixing—sexual or otherwise—and the representation of black political leaders at ease with a multiracial base of supporters, continues to stir emotional responses within African American communities, as in America as a whole. Interracial relationships—sexual, social, and otherwise—certainly played a significant role in shaping Obama's adult identity as a mixed-race African American male. During his university and law school years, Obama received important life lessons in the vagaries of interracial dating. He recounts an incident from his undergraduate days at Columbia University when his white girlfriend reacted negatively to a play with "typical black humor." As Obama recalls, his frustration boiled over after his girlfriend "started talking about why black people were so angry all the time."[88] The tendency that some white Americans have of seeing blacks as angry and interpreting the feelings and ideas of African American people as hostile toward the United States—and, as the Wright controversy reminded us, as unpatriotic—has been a source of black-white tension for generations. From white fears about slave insurrections, corrupt and cunning "mulatto" politicians during Reconstruction, and the violent condemnation of "uppity Negroes" during the Jim Crow era, to perceptions of radical, Marxist, and unpatriotic black leaders during the civil rights and Black Power movements in the 1960s and 1970s, African American leaders have struggled to unshackle themselves from negative racial perceptions. As Andrew Delbanco, a literary scholar, has observed, a number of white middle- and working-class people from midwestern and southern states "distrust [Obama's] verbal fluency and feel he is nothing more than a smooth-talking huckster."[89] Racialized views of this nature tap into a deep vein of historical distrust for African American leaders. As we noted earlier in this chapter, embedded in American political and popular history is a racialized language about cunning "mulatto" and black politicians that draws on phrases such as "inexperienced," "lacking competence," "aggressive," and "left-wing," and cues memories of the allegedly corrupt era of Reconstruction and the uncomfortable social, cultural, and political changes inspired by the civil rights movement in the 1950s and 1960s.[90]

Barack Obama's atypical childhood, his foreign-sounding name, and his mixed-race identity have exposed the racial tensions that simmer beneath the thin veneer of American politeness and "postracial" rhetoric. Obama is aware of the United States' racial past, but as a political leader, he strives to unite all Americans by drawing on America's national mythos. This is why his March 18, 2008, speech in Philadelphia started with his reiteration of the Founding Fathers' commitment to the creation of "a more perfect union." It is also why, in July 2008, Obama claimed that the republic's Founders did not fight for political independence from the British "on behalf of a particular tribe or lineage, but on behalf of a larger idea. The idea of liberty. The idea of God-given, inalienable rights."[91] These are the words of a patriotic American; they are also words that appeal to a mythology of the United States' founding, a reverential language that can make deeper analysis and understanding of race and mixed-race issues in America difficult for those who don't wish to appear to be unpatriotic, radical, or worse, "playing the race card."

In the following two sections of this chapter, we explore in greater detail the racial implications attached to the political history of which Obama is now a major part. While Obama overcame misgivings among African Americans about his "blackness," a nagging suspicion that he is opportunistic, foreign, and, as Sarah Palin quipped, "does not see America the way you and I do" continued to be articulated among some white Americans until November 2008.[92] In this sense, old fears about a cunning and self-aggrandizing "mulatto" politician persisted; that these racial ideas failed to prevent Obama from winning the White House was testimony to the Republican Party's lack of vision during the 2008 campaign, and to the racial advances that have been made in the United States since the civil rights movement.[93]

American Politics since the Civil War

In the years following General Robert E. Lee's surrender to General Ulysses S. Grant at Appomattox Court House on April 9, 1865, an event that marked the official end of the American Civil War, a number of black, "mulatto," and formerly enslaved African Americans entered national, state, and local politics for the first time. In a postwar era characterized by bloody violence, Blanche K. Bruce, John Mercer Langston, Robert Smalls, and other brave black politicians overcame white intimidation to be among the first African Americans elected to the United States Congress.[94] At the state and local level, men such as P. B. S. Pinchback, who became the governor of Louisiana in 1872, defied white vigilante violence to win elective office. All of these men endured public barbs about their racial heritage, lack of political experience, supposedly questionable character, and general incompetence. Blanche K. Bruce, for instance, was accused of being corrupt and "more fool than knave."[95] Pinchback, by contrast, was described as "not darker than an Arab," and having a disturbingly "restless glance," "sardonic smile," and "evil look."[96]

These racial epithets followed African American politicians into the twentieth century and are strikingly similar to those directed at Barack Obama during his 2008 presidential campaign. Obama's experience, character, and family background all faced intense, often mean-spirited, public scrutiny and ridicule. For instance, the former mayor of New York City, Rudolph Giuliani, mocked Obama's work as a community organizer—work that focused on poor, predominantly African American neighborhoods on the South Side of Chicago—at the 2008 Republican National Convention. Giuliani referred to Obama as "a gifted man with an Ivy League education. He worked as a community organizer.

[guffaws] What? He worked—I said—I said, OK, OK, maybe this is the first problem on the resume."[97] It is not unusual for a political candidate's experience and ability to face scrutiny from more seasoned political opponents (especially when those opponents are struggling to articulate coherent policy objectives), but the venomous nature with which Obama's work experience and his former associates were questioned reflected a political tradition of belittling and viciously attacking black politicians that dates back to the Reconstruction era of the late 1860s and 1870s, and that continued in different forms through to the civil rights movement.

In the preceding chapter, we demonstrated that slave religion, to quote from the theological scholars Dwight Hopkins and George Cummings, provided black Americans with "a liberated space in which slaves controlled the political power to develop their [own] theology."[98] After the Civil War and the emancipation of the South's slaves, the black church provided worshippers with an opportunity to express their harsher criticisms of American democracy. The black church, in short, was the foundation of African American politics and social activism. For those black Americans who entered the "mainstream" of American politics during Reconstruction, the black church's critique of American democracy's failures was measured against the need to provide leadership for millions of newly emancipated and impoverished African Americans in a predominantly white world. During the early years of Reconstruction, black ministers, military men, and a large population of skilled and unskilled craftsmen and laborers—men we would refer to today as "working-class"—entered the rough-and-tumble arena of postbellum politics. Black politicians worked to disabuse white Americans of the notion that African Americans constituted a homogenous mass of degraded people.[99] Black Americans therefore saw political participation as a route to legal equality and social acceptance in the United States—what Obama referred to as the pursuit of "a more perfect union" in his Philadelphia speech—and the Freedmen's Bureau encouraged black political participation. For example, General Rufus Saxton, a Freedmen's Bureau official in South Carolina, wrote: "I want the colored men in this department to petition the President of the United States and Congress for the right to exercise the elective franchise—the right to vote for those who are to rule over them."[100]

Black Americans had been active in American politics prior to the late 1860s and 1870s, as men such as Frederick Douglass (who was the Equal Rights Party's vice-presidential nominee in 1872) lobbied for the abolition of slavery in the decades prior to the Civil War.[101] However, Reconstruction politics was different, as the right to vote and elect black representatives held the potential to change the political landscape of the South and move the United States a step closer to the ideal of "a more perfect union." The prospect of black political leadership terrified the white South, most southerners viewing the federal government's Reconstruction policies, in either their radical or conservative form, as grotesque social-engineering experiments designed to create an unnatural social environment characterized by racial equality and permanent Republican Party rule.[102]

Black Americans, however, expressed an unshakable determination to participate in American political life, most seeing civic participation as a positive means of shaping the future destiny of their race.[103] Obama praised these and subsequent black leaders in his "A More Perfect Union" speech, stating that "through protests and struggles, on the streets and in the courts, through a civil war and civil disobedience and always at great risk," black (and white) Americans have often launched sustained efforts "to narrow the gap between the promise of our ideals and the reality of their time."[104] For black Americans who have risen to the challenge of political leadership since the Civil War, involvement in public service has meant an opportunity to encourage "race pride" in former slaves and their descendents. "Race pride" has meant different things to different people over the past century and a half. To black politicians like Oscar

De Priest, the first African American congressman in the U.S. House of Representatives in the twentieth century, "race pride" meant political participation and equality before the law.[105] For other black Americans, "race pride" involved blacks being able to negotiate the terms of labor contracts, a "self-help" ethos made famous by Booker T. Washington.[106] "Race pride" has represented a way for black Americans to endeavor to overcome racist stereotypes about black sexuality, black corruption, and black incompetence.[107]

Black political equality, however, made a majority of white Americans in both the North and the South uncomfortable. Many whites expressed derision, anger, and despair at the thought of sharing legal equality with blacks, and gave voice to a sense of utter terror at the prospect of the "misguided negroes [who are] corrupt and ignorant men" participating in national political life.[108] Similar, albeit attenuated, perceptions dogged Obama during his 2008 campaign. However, just how much race relations have improved can be gauged by returning to the years immediately after the Civil War. For example, John Yule of Placer County, California, articulated the humiliation that many whites felt after losing political power to former slaves: "It is 'nigger' in the Hall of Congress, 'nigger' in the camps of our armies, 'nigger' in the legislature of California, 'nigger' everywhere! The everlasting 'nigger' permeates the whole atmosphere of the entire country. He has arrived in our legislative halls at last."[109] During the 1860s and 1870s, multiracial political gatherings were lampooned as "black and tan convention[s]" that were also attended by white "carpetbaggers" and "nigger worshippers."[110] Such crude racial language was thankfully absent in political attacks on Obama's multiracial bid for the presidency, though the publication of the song "Barack the Magic Negro" by the conservative comedian Paul Shanklin suggests racist satires have not been completely eliminated from American society.[111]

What lingering racism remains in the United States has,

according to journalistic reports, been linked to the socioeconomic hardships of working-class Americans. Obama has addressed these reports, noting in his "A More Perfect Union" speech, as elsewhere, that the recent history of "welfare and affirmative action helped forge the Reagan coalition." Obama added that "talk show hosts and conservative commentators built entire careers unmasking bogus claims of racism while dismissing legitimate discussions of racial injustice and inequality as mere political correctness or reverse racism."[112] In his Philadelphia speech, and throughout the 2008 campaign, Obama had to walk a fine line between appeasing white working-class voters and acknowledging the continuing socioeconomic impact of past racism. With words that likely made some white listeners wince, Obama argued that "in the white community, the path to a more perfect union means acknowledging that what ails the African American community does not just exist in the minds of black people; that the legacy of discrimination—and current incidents of discrimination, while less overt than in the past—are real and must be addressed."[113]

The racial history that Obama referred to in his "A More Perfect Union" speech emphasized the interrelated ways in which racism, class, and socioeconomic opportunities (or lack of opportunities) have often been woven together to disadvantage black Americans. In the wake of slavery's abolition, for example, white racial beliefs in both the North and South self-servingly held that black workers preferred to steal and cheat white employers than put in an honest day's labor. One ex-Confederate colonel expressed this belief succinctly: "As for the niggers . . . [t]hey won't work, unless you force them to it, and they'll steal rather than starve."[114] Views of this nature were an important component of the racial common sense of the postbellum South. Moreover, such beliefs complemented the sexual stereotypes about black people by insisting that African Americans must be contained through their labor as sharecroppers and unskilled laborers. What scholars refer to as the "etiquette of race relations" in the South thus presaged the white working class's disdain for what they saw as the "mad philanthropy" of missionaries and Reconstruction politicians. In the minds of working-class and poorer whites in the late nineteenth and early twentieth centuries, the "mad philanthropy" of private and government institutions handed black laborers special advantages that were not available to struggling whites.[115]

The white poor and working-class perception of special privileges for black labor—what we today refer to as "affirmative action"—prompted one nineteenth-century commentator to engage in a specious rewriting of history: "The negro is unfortunate . . . *but* in the country of the whites where the labor of whites has done everything, but his [African American] labor nothing, and where the whites find it difficult to earn a subsistence, what right has the negro either to preference, or to equality, or to admission?"[116] So outraged did the white poor and working class become at the thought of legal and economic equality with blacks (something that labor unions and white workers articulated as "special privileges" for black workers) that, between 1882 and 1900, southern white workers went on strike fifty times to protest the employment of black labor.[117]

In postbellum America, members of the white working class also expressed their resentment of black workers because former slaves actively competed for wage-labor positions. Many union leaders pandered to these perceptions, arguing that the "true station of the negro is that of servant. The wants of state and country demand that he should remain a servant."[118] By the twentieth century, white workers and labor leaders rationalized their opposition to equality with black labor by insisting that African American workers retarded the progress of the working class by allowing themselves to be employed as "'cheap men,' and all realize that 'cheap men' are not only an impediment to the attainment of the workers' just rights, and the progress of civilization, but will tie themselves to the slough of despond and despair."[119]

The white working class's deep-rooted historical suspicion of black workers and black political leaders reared its ugly head during Obama's 2008 campaign for the presidency. For all the excuses that white working-class voters gave for not supporting Obama's candidacy, racism remained behind the working-class hostility. Marc Ambinder, the associate editor of the *Atlantic,* captured the tenor of contemporary racism among white working-class voters in his account of a 2008 speech by Richard Trumka, the AFL-CIO's secretary-treasurer:

> Trumka spoke about an encounter he'd had during the Democratic primaries. "I went back to my hometown in Nemacolin [Pennsylvania], and I ran into a woman that I've . . . known for years. She was active in Democratic politics when I was still in grade school." The woman told Trumka that she was voting for Hillary Clinton. "'There's no way that I'd ever vote for Obama.' I said, 'Why is that?' She said, 'Well, he's Muslim.' And I said, 'Well, actually, he's Christian, just like you and I. But so what if he's Muslim?' Then she shook her head and said, 'Well, he won't wear that American-flag pin on his lapel.'" Trumka told her that Obama did, indeed, wear a flag pin. Then she said, "'Well, I just don't trust him.' . . . She drops her voice a bit. And she says, 'Because he's black.'"[120]

Racial prejudice still exists among white working-class Americans, just as it exists in various forms among other socioeconomic groups in American society. These prejudices, however, no longer carry the same electoral weight that they carried during the early twentieth century, or even a generation ago.

This change occurred because, during World War II and the decades of the civil rights movement, black newspaper editors, black ministers and church members, and an articulate group of African American union organizers and lawyers led a social movement that changed American race relations for the better. Obama praised these people in his "A More Perfect Union" speech, referring to their acts of "civil disobedience" that transformed America. The brave Americans Obama referred to included the editors of the *Pittsburgh Courier*'s Double V campaign during World War II; African American union leaders like A. Phillip Randolph; and black ministers like Martin Luther King Jr. As a result, civil rights activism unleashed, as Roy Wilkins, the former leader of the NAACP, observed, "a ridiculous, ignorant fear of black Americans."[121]

In the decades following the Second World War, African Americans used a variety of tactics to overcome "ignorant fear," to lobby for civil rights, and to pave the way for black men and women like Obama to play a prominent role in late twentieth- and early twenty-first-century politics. From black workers threatening to march on Washington during World War II, to African American boycotts of consumer items such as the American Tobacco Company's "Nigger Hair" tobacco and Whiteman Candy Company's "Pickaninny Chocolate," to the sit-ins, marches, and political protests led by black Americans like Martin Luther King Jr., white Americans were forced to engage in a liberal program of reform that led to the dismantling of the Jim Crow system.[122] As Obama has acknowledged, his political success is "a pure product of that era" of civil rights reform.[123]

In his books and speeches, Obama has acknowledged that the struggles of the civil rights movement continue to shape how millions of black Americans understand issues such as housing discrimination, poverty, and unemployment. In *The Audacity of Hope*, Obama argued that "for all the progress that's been made in the past four decades, a stubborn gap remains between the living standards of black, Latino, and white workers."[124] Reverend Wright's sermons were filled with similar cautionary statements about the extent to which racial progress has actually been achieved in the United States, just as Martin Luther King Jr. before him lamented that black Americans experience, more than any other group, "a lonely island of economic insecurity in the midst of a vast ocean of material prosperity."[125]

The legacy of political activism and the sense of social justice that King's legacy bequeathed to future generations of black Americans like Obama were deeply indebted to the quest for a sense of community and Christian charity. King's speeches were far less idealistic than they are now remembered as being: he regularly criticized white "tokenism"—an underpaid job here, a solitary black politician there—toward black Americans. For Obama, who is a product of post–civil rights movement America, King's message of political activism and social justice demands a renewed commitment from all Americans. Obama's 2008 campaign and the early months of his presidency have been defined by an effort to reframe racial debates in politics, an effort that targets "conservatives [who] won over white public opinion . . . [with] arguments that tapped into a distinction between the 'deserving' and 'undeserving' poor . . . , an argument that has often been racially and ethnically tinged."[126] Thus, Obama views the right-wing assault on the gains made in race relations during the civil rights movement as a threat to the democratic principles of the United States. The racially charged—and often racist—attack on civil rights reform led Obama into work as a community organizer and, ultimately, into state and national politics.

The right-wing attack on the legacy of the civil rights movement helps to explain both the difficulties that Obama had in winning white working-class votes during 2008 and the often-hateful language used by some white voters to describe Obama. These attacks—evident in claims that Obama is inexperienced, is a Muslim, refuses to wear an American flag pin on his lapel—were coded ways for white Americans to say that they were uncomfortable voting for a black man for president. White hostility and distrust of black political leaders received renewed focus during the civil rights movement, and became a "mainstream" concern with the rise of Black Power and that movement's attendant "black pride" slogans in the 1960s and 1970s.[127] Black Power mantras terrified white Americans, but these slogans arose from a set of conservative beliefs, practices, and cultural and religious expressions designed to provide African Americans protection and comfort in the face of what appeared to be the hostile world of whites. Obama has acknowledged the emotional appeal of black nationalism, but has also cautioned that such ideologies do not offer any political solution to the socioeconomic problems facing contemporary black Americans. In *Dreams from My Father,* Obama wrote that black nationalism and "black rage" involve "conspiracy theories . . . [such as that] the Koreans were funding the Klan, [and] Jewish doctors were injecting black babies with the AIDS virus." According to Obama, these conspiracy theories demonstrate "how [black] nationalism could thrive as an emotion and flounder as a program."[128] In shunning black nationalism, Obama highlights how his politics are in the liberal integrationist tradition of Martin Luther King Jr. and the civil rights movement.

Not all black Americans subscribe to one form or another of black nationalism. Cultural expression among black Americans is as diverse as it is among white, Asian, Hispanic, and indigenous Americans. Nevertheless, since the first stirrings of contemporary black nationalism in the late 1960s, many white Americans have felt that expressions like "black power" and "black pride"—and, in fact, any remarks that African Americans utter in criticism of the United States—constitute examples of militant "antiwhite racism." Obama has written about his personal experiences with these sentiments; he has also acknowledged that the civil rights movement and subsequent celebration of "multiculturalism" in American society has unleashed an anti–civil rights era backlash that a small but vocal segment of white Americans continues to embrace. Since the late 1960s, a number of white Americans have expressed discomfort about being, in their minds, under siege from "political correctness" and affirmative action schemes (and increasingly, a globalizing labor market in which manufacturing jobs are lost to Latin American and Asian countries). While most Americans happily partake in the frivolities of multiculturalism—enjoying exotic foods, foreign dance, and international films—the goodwill demonstrated in these activities has not always extended to the sharing of political power and a democratic redistribution of economic resources. In fact, a shrill segment of "conservative" America views any political and economic redistribution schemes as "reverse racism," and thus as harmful to honest, hardworking, white Americans.[129]

White claims of "reverse racism" have represented one of the more common responses to the civil rights era. Since the late 1960s, black political candidates like Obama have struggled to reassure white voters that they do not have an agenda to extend what some white Americans perceive are the excesses of the 1960s and the "reverse racism" of institutional policies that try to address historically disadvantaged people. Strom Thurmond, the long-serving United States senator from South Carolina, articulated these anxieties in the late 1960s, claiming: "We are now at a point [in American history] where depravity is fresh and likeable, whereas virtue is apparently false and insane."[130] Civil rights protests, women's rights activism, and the beginnings of a gay rights movement meant the death knell, Americans like Thurmond feared, for "traditional" American values. The threat that some Americans felt Obama posed to "traditional" American values in 2008—because he was thought to be a Muslim, not a "natural-born American," and politically radical—echoed the rhetoric of the white backlash to civil rights reform in the 1960s. In both the North and South, for example, Martin Luther King Jr., the most prominent civil rights leader of the 1950s and 1960s, was labeled a "communist," derided as "Martin Luther Coon," and accused in 1965 by a *U.S. News & World Report* journalist of being a "radical" who wanted to establish "a totalitarian state."[131] On the streets of the South and, when King moved to Chicago in 1966, the North, Confederate flags and placards that read "Roses are red, violets are black, King would look good with a knife in his back" followed King and other civil rights leaders in their quest for social justice.[132] King, like Obama, embodied to some whites the "uppity Negro," acting in a politically assertive way that threatened a way of life that was once defined by Jim Crow segregation, lynchings, disenfranchisement, and grinding poverty in black communities.

The 2008 publicity over Reverend Wright's sermons therefore evoked images of 1960s black radicalism that white Americans still find discomfiting. One of the key questions for millions of white voters became whether Obama shared Wright's views. After all, Obama and his wife, as thousands of Internet bloggers were at pains to emphasize, attended Wright's church for two decades. In spite of Obama's rejection of Wright's more incendiary comments in his "A More Perfect Union" speech, many conservative Americans attempted to smear Obama by labeling him an "urban radical," a caricature designed to evoke frightening images of the young, Afro-haired, dashiki-wearing, militant-sounding black men and women who antagonized the white working class and terrified the middle class in the late 1960s and 1970s. Since Barry Goldwater's failed bid for the White House in 1964, the Republican Party has exploited these racial fears among white voters by perfecting what scholars refer to as "wedge politics." Wedge politics involves the portrayal of the 1960s as a decade of radicalism, hedonism, and amoral excess; these caricatures also endeavor to demonize the Democratic Party as a party of tax-and-spend "do-gooders," in contrast to the Republican Party, which is portrayed as standing for "traditional," "small-town" American values and as working to shield hardworking Americans from pernicious "cultural issues." For example, Republican Party strategists have criticized "activist judges," "affirmative action," "gay marriage," and "pro-choice" supporters as examples of how traditional American values remain under siege by left-wing liberals.[133] Republican Party leaders and conservative commentators, as Obama has noted, claimed to be differentiating "mainstream" American values—the values of what Richard Nixon called the "great silent majority"—from the morally corrosive and social destabilizing reforms of the 1960s.[134] Significantly, conservative strategists have achieved this rearticulation of American political discourse by appealing to the racism of white working- and middle-class Americans. To this end, Republican strategists from the Nixon presidency to Ronald Reagan, George H. W. Bush, and George W. Bush have made calculated use of phrases like "states' rights," "political correctness run amok," "tax-and-spend Democrats," "welfare queens," "young bucks" exploiting food stamps, and "activist judges" who turn a blind eye to lawlessness on America's streets.[135] A former aide to President George H. W. Bush described the use of such rhetoric in Republican propaganda. Willie Horton—a convicted black sex offender who had been furloughed in Massachusetts under the governorship of Michael Dukakis, the 1988 Democratic presidential candidate—was portrayed in Republican Party advertisements as an example of liberal political excess that conveyed, in the words of the former Bush aide, "a wonderful mix of liberalism and a big black rapist."[136]

The Horton advertisement highlighted how Republican strategists have unscrupulously used color-conscious and racially charged images to win political office. To deflect charges of racism, Republican Party leaders pay lip service to vague notions of "color blindness." "Color blindness," which had once been liberal America's clarion call for racial justice, was transformed in the 1970s and 1980s into a conservative political attack on civil rights–era reforms under the guise of lowering taxes, slashing big government, and restoring "race neutrality" to American society.[137] Obama has expressed his skepticism about "color blindness" and the notion that race no longer disadvantages millions of Americans. As Obama argued in *The Audacity of Hope,* the civil rights movement did not completely emancipate the United States from the historical legacy of racism, nor should an uncritical embrace of "color blindness"—and "postracialism," for that matter—seduce people into thinking uncritically about the continued legacies of race and racism. As Obama argued, "To think clearly about race, then, requires us to see the world on a split screen—to maintain in our sights the kind of America that we want while looking squarely at America as it is."[138] "Color blindness," in other words, prohibits such sophisticated and mature approaches to discussions of race in America.

Obama, Race, and Politics

In two stunningly well-written books, *Dreams from My Father* (1995) and *The Audacity of Hope* (2006), Barack Obama provided clues to how as president he might engage Americans in a meaningful dialogue on race. These two books are more than personal narratives because they demonstrate the depth of Obama's understanding of the complexities of American race relations and the role of the black church in African American politics. In *Dreams from My Father*, for example, Obama recalled that as a community organizer on the South Side of Chicago, he wanted to unite the many black churches in the city. In Obama's mind, such unity would foster social and economic betterment in black Chicago. Obama thus recognized the value of faith communities in political efforts to create better social and economic worlds. For Obama, the black church was, as it had been for African American leaders before him, the core institution in his struggle for social justice on the South Side of Chicago.[139]

Obama joined Reverend Jeremiah Wright's Trinity United Church of Christ when he was in his mid-twenties. We have already discussed Obama's relationship with Wright and Trinity, but politically, it was one of Wright's sermons that captured Obama's imagination. In "The Audacity to Hope," Wright condemned abuses of political power and ongoing racism in American society, and drew on biblical messages of hope to inspire optimism in his congregation. Obama recalled that the sermon simplified many complex social and political issues, but that the power of the sermon was the way Wright provided a sense of community and hope for the future. With wonderfully rhythmic prose, Obama recalled Wright’s sermon:

> Our trials and triumphs became at once unique and universal, black and more than black; in chronicling our journey, the stories and songs gave us a means to reclaim memories that we didn’t need to feel ashamed about, memories more accessible than those of ancient Egypt, memories that all people might study and cherish—and with which we could start to rebuild.[140]

Wright’s “Audacity to Hope” sermon crystallized for Obama an optimistic vision of a better United States, an outlook on life that Obama’s mother had originally given to her son, and that Obama himself has taken into the White House. Sitting in Trinity United Church that Sunday morning, Obama felt connected not to a “color-blind” or “postracial” community of Americans, but to an America historically defined by racial fissures. Only through reflection and a genuine understanding of the complex issues associated with race and racism can all Americans work together to build “a more perfect union.”

Obama’s understanding of American race relations combines the optimism of an immigrant’s son, his Christian faith, and the harsh realities of the racialized poverty and discrimination that he witnessed as a community organizer on the South Side of Chicago. Even though his parents and grandparents did not endure the injustices of Jim Crow America, Obama’s keen intellect and his compassion for the suffering of others make him quick to caution against an uncritical acceptance of theories like “postracialism.”[141] In *The Audacity of Hope*, Obama argued: “To say that we are one people is not to suggest that race no longer matters—that the fight for equality has been won, or that the problems that minorities face in this country today are largely self-inflicted.”[142] As we have argued, the civil rights movement helped to improve American race relations. However, Obama knows that history does not unfold in a linear and continuously progressive fashion. Indeed, change does not always mean progress and a better standard of living for all Americans. In the context of three decades of white backlash against the civil rights era, Obama recognizes that "more minorities may be living the American dream, but their hold on that dream remains tenuous."[143]

As Obama's political career gathered momentum in the last decade, he, like other African American politicians (Cory Booker in Newark, New Jersey, and Deval Patrick in Massachusetts), mediated for white audiences the harsher critiques of American racism that are traditionally heard in black churches, barber shops, and around African American dinner tables. As one reporter recently put it, Obama is "black, but not too black"; that is, not black enough to frighten non–African American voters, some of whom continue to associate black leadership with negative images of militant civil rights and Black Power leaders.[144] Obama, Booker, and Patrick embody the new black politician: they are highly educated and articulate; they form political coalitions and alliances that cross racial lines; and, perhaps most importantly, they lack the racial baggage that many whites associate with figures like Al Sharpton and Jesse Jackson.[145] Obama's message of self-help and personal responsibility, and his professed faith in the power of American institutions to unite all Americans, may sound to some like a rearticulation of Booker T. Washington's self help ethos, but unlike Washington (who caused outrage when he dined with President Theodore Roosevelt at the White House in 1901), Obama entered the Oval Office unflinching in his self-identification as a black American man. As his "A More Perfect Union" speech and past writings suggest, President Obama appears determined not to ignore long-standing racial divisions.[146]

Obama's "A More Perfect Union" speech helped to frame his 2008 campaign. The speech was also an eloquent example of resurgent liberalism in the United States. Recognizing "this nation's original sin of slavery," Obama eschewed discussion of the coded racial rhetoric and hostility to civil rights reform that has dominated political debate for the past generation. Instead, he sought to reframe political debates about race by rearticulating America's commitment to the ideal "of equal citizenship under the law." For the past two decades, conservatives have used the concept of "equality before the law" as part of a self-serving attempt to roll back civil rights reform in the name of "color blindness." Obama's liberalism puts a twenty-first-century spin on civil rights era reforms. This reminder of the limits of "color blindness" and "postracialism" was one of the major points of this and other speeches Obama has made. As Obama stated in Philadelphia, "the disparities that exist in African American communities today can be directly traced to inequalities that have been reluctantly passed on from earlier generations who suffered under the brutal legacy of slavery and Jim Crow."[147]

While Obama acknowledged in his "A More Perfect Union" speech that the effects of racism continue to shape the lives of millions of Americans, he also recognized that as a candidate for the Democratic Party's presidential nomination, he had to walk a fine line in highlighting both the racial basis for many of America's continuing social and economic ills and the negative impact that the loss of manufacturing jobs has had on the white working class.[148] Obama stated: "Most working- and middle-class white Americans don't feel that they have been particularly privileged by their race. Their experience is the immigrant experience—as far as they're concerned, no one's handed them anything, they've built it from scratch. They've worked hard all their lives, many times only to see their jobs shipped overseas or their pension dumped after a lifetime of labor."[149] Obama's comments, politically calibrated as they may have been, reflected his acknowledgment that if he wanted to have any chance of becoming president of the United States, a rhetorical balancing act was necessary to prevent the alienation of his black base and to build political coalitions with white working-class voters.[150]

Just as it was difficult for candidate Obama to forge interracial coalitions, it may be no easier for President Obama to bridge the racial divides that continue to separate Americans. The tenor of public debate during the 2008 presidential election was indicative of the racial hostility that Obama and his supporters may encounter during his presidency. In the wake of Reverend Wright's appearance at the National Press Club, a *New York Times* political forum addressed Obama's relationship with Reverend Wright. One correspondent to this forum criticized Wright, and Barack and Michelle Obama, with words that captured the rightward shift in American racial politics over the past generation:

> I guess that "white" people are his enemy then as "they" put "him?" in chains. A rant of an angry man who sees "white devils" instead of just people. The only chain I see on him is a gold wristwatch. The problem is that his messages of hate have been accepted by Obama and wife for many years now. I would have and I have left churches that preach the hate of "them" or "those other people". This disturbing image is brought home also in Obama's wife comments that just now she has somethng to be proud of America about??? Wow. I've been proud of this country and its people on more than one occaison. I believe that people I know would say the same. They are "out of touch."[151]

The above quotation reflects a tendency among some Americans to view outspoken black leaders like Wright as a relic from a bygone era, as angry men who play "the race card" to line their own pockets (a point suggested by the reference to Wright's "gold wristwatch"). The blogger quoted above adds, in language that reverberates with the polarizing rhetoric of Nixon's "great silent majority" speech, that because Barack and Michelle Obama have had a two-decade-long relationship with Reverend Wright (and because Obama expressed polite empathy for what he saw as Wright's outmoded stance on race relations), they must be "out of touch" with real, hardworking, patriotic Americans.[152] Here the blogger is reacting to Michelle Obama's statement that seeing her husband run for president of the United States made her feel "for the first time in my adult lifetime . . . really proud of my country."[153] Far from being "out of touch," Michelle Obama's remarks were those of a rational, thoughtful black woman, a woman who has lived with the realities of race in America, and who, understandably, is not proud of the United States' history with slavery, segregation, and the political backlash against the civil rights movement. Michelle Obama, like her husband, does not subscribe to a message of hate, nor is she "out of touch"; rather, the Obamas belong to a long tradition—from Frederick Douglass's struggle for the abolition of slavery to Martin Luther King Jr.'s quest for civil rights—of black Americans who challenge America to live up to its lofty ideals and work to create "a more perfect union."

Obama's victory over John McCain on November 4, 2008, came in spite of lingering racial resentment in America. Across the country, the less-educated, white working-class constituency that the Republican Party has explicitly claimed to represent since Reagan's presidency repeatedly told Obama campaign workers that "he is black," "I don't trust him," "he is an Arab," "he is a Muslim," "he was not born in America," and he "is going to push black values."[154] The continued use of these epithets suggests that a number of Americans in post–civil rights movement America continue to feel besieged by "political correctness." As a result, those who feel uncertain about the twenty-first-century times in which they live display a tendency to resort to racial slurs against black leaders. But progress has been made since the days of Reconstruction. In a small town in Ohio, for example, a twenty-three-year-old white woman told a British reporter less than a month before the general election that she was going to vote for Obama even though he "looks foreign and he looks like a terrorist."[155]

Conclusion

Americans tend to think of their past, particularly the founding of the American republic, as an epic tale of democratic triumph over colonial despots. The uncommon wisdom of the Founding Fathers, American mythology tells us, emancipated the colonies from the Old World, setting the United States apart from all other nations in its pursuit of life, liberty, and happiness.[156] However, since the Declaration of Independence in 1776 and the ratification of the United States Constitution, the ideals of American democracy have often been undermined by race and racism. Race has proven to be the central fissure in American society, its "scavenger nature," as a number of recent scholars point out, making it possible for racial meanings to be reinscribed with each new generation of Americans.[157] Perhaps this is why Obama has insisted that the Constitution of the United States must be seen as the framework for an ongoing conversation about the meaning of American democracy. As Obama contends in *The Audacity of Hope*, such a conversation will embody "a 'deliberative democracy' in which all citizens are required to engage in a process of testing their ideas against an external reality."[158]

Obama entered the White House in January 2009 with the "postracial" hopes of millions of Americans resting on his shoulders. Could the first black man to occupy the Oval Office lead Americans into a future in which race no longer figures in American life? Such questions remain to be answered, but no matter what the future holds, racial progress (which can mean different things to different people) must involve a serious and sensitive grappling with America's past. Obama may prove the catalyst for such discussions; he and his family certainly embody the contradictions of race relations in American history, a history characterized by slavery, immigration, interracial marriage, mixed-race identity, periods of interracial cooperation, and perhaps most importantly since the terrorist attacks of September 11, 2001, the different ways Americans choose to celebrate their democracy. If nothing else, the 2008 presidential election demonstrated, to borrow from the journalist Patricia Williams, how public debate about race and racism "ricochets between hypersensitivity and oblivion."[159] Perhaps, just perhaps, the racial history that President Obama embodies will help Americans mediate these two emotional polarities and finally engage in a meaningful, mature, and democratic discussion of America's racial history.

"To Choose Our Better History"?

Epilogue

On January 20, 2009, Barack H. Obama was sworn in as the forty-fourth president of the United States. A million or so people, from throughout the United States and abroad, crammed onto the Washington Mall to glimpse history in the making: the inauguration of the first African American president of the United States. Television and newspaper journalists reported seeing tears of joy and hearing whoops of excitement from members of the massive crowd as Obama delivered his inaugural speech.[1] For a generation of African Americans who had struggled for civil rights in the 1950s and 1960s, Obama's inauguration was particularly special. To this generation of Americans, many now in their sixties and seventies, Obama's presidency represented a high point in black America's historical struggle to transform America's ideals of equality and social justice into a reality.[2] In addressing the million or so people on the Washington Mall, Obama captured the hopes of generations past when he urged Americans "to choose our better history."[3]

Obama's words echoed Abraham Lincoln's call for Americans to live according to "the better angels of our nature."[4] Indeed, the link between Lincoln and Obama was palpable in the days leading up to the inauguration. Obama, for example, chose to arrive in the capital by retracing portions of Lincoln's train journey from Illinois to Washington, D.C. (although Obama, unlike Lincoln, did not have to arrive in secret for fear of being assassinated by southern extremists). Obama also used Lincoln's Bible at the swearing-in ceremony; and he repeated the inaccurate claim that Lincoln freed the slaves (something that was achieved in December 1865 by the Thirteenth Amendment to the U.S. Constitution), by implication linking himself to the great white emancipator of the Civil War era.[5] Historical inaccuracies aside, the Lincoln-Obama imagery was designed to unite Americans; just as Lincoln contributed to the downfall of racial slavery and reunited the South with the North, so Obama is seen by millions of Americans as the best hope of restoring cohesion to a nation that is divided over the "war on terror," wracked by economic uncertainty, and anxious about racial and ethnic issues such as immigration restriction, the ongoing fallout from Hurricane Katrina, and urban poverty. For young Americans (eighteen- to twenty-nine-year-olds), Obama embodies a "postracial" departure from America's sordid political and racial past. For the civil rights generation, Obama puts a modern spin on the liberal reform for which thousands marched, sat in, and protested in the 1950s and 1960s. Thus, to black Americans who live with the memories of the civil rights movement, Obama's presidency represents less a "postracial" departure from America's racial history than a new phase in the ongoing struggle to transform the ideals of the Founders into a reality for all. Americans will no doubt continue to debate the meaning of Obama's presidency, but if his election says anything about the United States, it is that the republic is not a white nation, but a multiracial society.

While Obama's inaugural address drew on some powerful historical imagery, his caution as a politician, his studied understanding of America's racial history, and his cautious approach to the challenges facing the United States over the next four years led him to celebrate American idealism in measured tones. In fact, Obama's address reflected both his skill as a politician and his understanding of the complexities of history; the speech made it clear that faith in America's founding ideals must unite Americans, while at the same time recognizing the importance of history's lessons in guiding America's future. As Obama instructed the Inauguration Day crowds:

> We are a nation of Christians and Muslims, Jews and Hindus, and nonbelievers. We are shaped by every language and culture, drawn from every end of this Earth.
>
> And because we have tasted the bitter swill of civil war and segregation and emerged from that dark chapter stronger and more united, we cannot help but believe that the old hatreds shall someday pass; that the lines of tribe shall soon dissolve; that as the world grows smaller, our common humanity shall reveal itself.[6]

One could, if one wanted to, read into these words the "post-racial" idealism that Americans still find hard to adequately articulate. We read Obama's words as evidence of a skillful politician holding out hope to those who need inspiration, while demonstrating to those who refuse to turn an uncritical eye to the continuing effects of American history that race, and moments of racism, continue to threaten the meaningful fulfillment of the Founding Fathers' ideals. This admonition, like the jeremiads of his former pastor the Reverend Jeremiah Wright, reflects an understanding of the malformative role race and racism have played in American history.

If nothing else, Wright's sermons reminded Americans that daily life in some black communities is anything but "postracial." Exit poll data from the November 2008 election indicated that while racial divisions are no longer as entrenched as they once were, only a naïve optimist would argue that race no longer influences decision making in the United States. Data published by the *New York Times* suggest that 43 percent of white voters cast their ballot for Obama. This was the highest white vote for a Democratic candidate since 1976, when Jimmy Carter won the White House with 47 percent of the white, and 83 percent of the black, vote. The 2008 election, however, did not go to Obama because of white voters, but thanks to a coalition of black, Hispanic, and Asian American voters, with 95 percent of blacks, 67 percent of Hispanics, and 62 percent of Asian Americans voting for the Democratic ticket.[7] Many conclusions can be drawn from these statistics. On one hand, the data suggest that white and nonwhite Americans remain as politically divided as ever. On the other hand, the changing demographic nature of the United States (resulting, in some instances, in whites being an electoral minority) has the potential to change the nature of American politics over the next generation. Is this what Obama was referring to when he asserted that "the lines of tribe shall soon dissolve"? Perhaps. It does appear, however, that where lines of black and white once dominated American society, new lines of white and nonwhite are being redrawn and redefined for the twenty-first century. Understanding this racial remapping of American society will likely hold the key to political success as the century unfolds.

There is another possibility for the future that is as promising as it is potentially terrifying. Exit polling showed that 66 percent of eighteen- to twenty-nine-year-olds voted for Obama in 2008. In comparison, 32 percent of Americans in this demographic voted for the Republican Party ticket. Is this the rising tide of a generational sea change in American politics in which the "wedge politics"—or what Obama called, in his inauguration speech, "worn-out dogmas"—no longer sway voters? Only time will tell, but it is significant that this demographic, and the generation following them, proclaim a categorical refusal to see race. The *New York Times* columnist Judith Warner wrote of her experience with new generations of Americans who feel that even celebrating Barack Obama as the first African American president of the United States is racist. Warner wrote that her eight-year-old daughter, Emilie, castigated her for "being racist" because she celebrated the profound historical meaning behind Obama's victory. In Emilie's words, "Why should it matter if people are black or white?"[8] Emilie had a valid point: race shouldn't matter in American society. The fact is, however, it does matter, for some more than others. To ignore distinctions between black and white Americans is not only to engage in the erasure of a central component of the United States' history, it is to deny the humanity of people like President Obama who claim for themselves an identity as black men or women in America.

When Martin Luther King Jr. stood before the Lincoln Memorial and proclaimed his "I Have a Dream" speech, he was not calling on Americans to forget the impact that race and racism were continuing to have on American society; instead, King's speech was a call for the United States to live up to its founding ideals so that black Americans like Barack Obama could one day share in real, tangible power: political power.[9] Obama's grasp on political power became tenuous after media reports surrounding his membership in Trinity United Church of Christ emerged. Until the Reverend Jeremiah Wright's sermons were made public, Obama's story was that of a mixed-race American who had succeeded beyond expectation in American society; the son of a white mother from Kansas and a black father from Kenya, Obama embodied for some Americans the ideal of a "postracial" America where "the lines of tribe shall soon dissolve." Obama's relationship with Wright compromised all this, emphasizing Obama's blackness, his foreignness, and his radicalism. For some Americans, Barack Obama became "the country's first mulatto president," determined to push "black values" on an unsuspecting public.[10] That these racial attacks failed to destroy Obama's bid for the White House is testimony to the racial advances that have occurred in the United States over the past half century. That such attacks are still articulated at all reflects the folly involved in turning our backs on America's racial history. Rather than viewing a black minister like Jeremiah Wright as some sort of unpatriotic extremist, and black churchgoers like Obama, who listen to sermons like Wright's each Sunday, as dangerous and foreign, some Americans must come to understand that a moral and critical patriotism is essential to the survival of the nation.

Barack Obama's Speech on Race

Delivered March 18, 2008, at the National Constitution Center in Philadelphia

"We the people, in order to form a more perfect union."

Two hundred and twenty-one years ago, in a hall that still stands across the street, a group of men gathered and, with these simple words, launched America's improbable experiment in democracy. Farmers and scholars; statesmen and patriots who had traveled across an ocean to escape tyranny and persecution finally made real their declaration of independence at a Philadelphia convention that lasted through the spring of 1787.

The document they produced was eventually signed but ultimately unfinished. It was stained by this nation's original sin of slavery, a question that divided the colonies and brought the convention to a stalemate until the founders chose to allow the slave trade to continue for at least twenty more years, and to leave any final resolution to future generations.

Of course, the answer to the slavery question was already

From the *New York Times*, March 18, 2008,

embedded within our Constitution—a Constitution that had at its very core the ideal of equal citizenship under the law; a Constitution that promised its people liberty, and justice, and a union that could be and should be perfected over time.

And yet words on a parchment would not be enough to deliver slaves from bondage, or provide men and women of every color and creed their full rights and obligations as citizens of the United States. What would be needed were Americans in successive generations who were willing to do their part—through protests and struggle, on the streets and in the courts, through a civil war and civil disobedience and always at great risk—to narrow that gap between the promise of our ideals and the reality of their time.

This was one of the tasks we set forth at the beginning of this campaign—to continue the long march of those who came before us, a march for a more just, more equal, more free, more caring, and more prosperous America. I chose to run for the presidency at this moment in history because I believe deeply that we cannot solve the challenges of our time unless we solve them together—unless we perfect our union by understanding that we may have different stories, but we hold common hopes; that we may not look the same and we may not have come from the same place, but we all want to move in the same direction—towards a better future for our children and our grandchildren.

This belief comes from my unyielding faith in the decency and generosity of the American people. But it also comes from my own American story.

I am the son of a black man from Kenya and a white woman from Kansas. I was raised with the help of a white grandfather who survived a Depression to serve in Patton's Army during World War II and a white grandmother who worked on a bomber assembly line at Fort Leavenworth while he was overseas. I've gone to some of the best schools in America and lived in one of the world's poorest nations. I am married to a black American who carries within her the blood of slaves and slaveow inheritance we pass on to our two precious daughters brothers, sisters, nieces, nephews, uncles, and cousins, of every race and every hue, scattered across three continents, and for as long as I live, I will never forget that in no other country on Earth is my story even possible.

It's a story that hasn't made me the most conventional candidate. But it is a story that has seared into my genetic makeup the idea that this nation is more than the sum of its parts—that out of many, we are truly one.

Throughout the first year of this campaign, against all predictions to the contrary, we saw how hungry the American people were for this message of unity. Despite the temptation to view my candidacy through a purely racial lens, we won commanding victories in states with some of the whitest populations in the country. In South Carolina, where the Confederate flag still flies, we built a powerful coalition of African Americans and white Americans.

This is not to say that race has not been an issue in the campaign. At various stages in the campaign, some commentators have deemed me either "too black" or "not black enough." We saw racial tensions bubble to the surface during the week before the South Carolina primary. The press has scoured every exit poll for the latest evidence of racial polarization, not just in terms of white and black, but black and brown as well.

And yet, it has only been in the last couple of weeks that the discussion of race in this campaign has taken a particularly divisive turn.

On one end of the spectrum, we've heard the implication that my candidacy is somehow an exercise in affirmative action; that it's based solely on the desire of wide-eyed liberals to purchase racial reconciliation on the cheap. On the other end, we've heard my former pastor, Reverend Jeremiah Wright, use incendiary language to express views that have the potential not only to widen the racial divide, but views that denigrate both the greatness and the goodness of our nation; that rightly offend white and black alike.

I have already condemned, in unequivocal terms, the statements of Reverend Wright that have caused such controversy. For some, nagging questions remain. Did I know him to be an occasionally fierce critic of American domestic and foreign policy? Of course. Did I ever hear him make remarks that could be considered controversial while I sat in church? Yes. Did I strongly disagree with many of his political views? Absolutely—just as I'm sure many of you have heard remarks from your pastors, priests, or rabbis with which you strongly disagreed.

But the remarks that have caused this recent firestorm weren't simply controversial. They weren't simply a religious leader's effort to speak out against perceived injustice. Instead, they expressed a profoundly distorted view of this country—a view that sees white racism as endemic, and that elevates what is wrong with America above all that we know is right with America; a view that sees the conflicts in the Middle East as rooted primarily in the actions of stalwart allies like Israel, instead of emanating from the perverse and hateful ideologies of radical Islam.

As such, Reverend Wright's comments were not only wrong but divisive, divisive at a time when we need unity; racially charged at a time when we need to come together to solve a set of monumental problems—two wars, a terrorist threat, a falling economy, a chronic health care crisis, and potentially devastating climate change; problems that are neither black or white or Latino or Asian, but rather problems that confront us all.

Given my background, my politics, and my professed values and ideals, there will no doubt be those for whom my statements of condemnation are not enough. Why associate myself with Reverend Wright in the first place, they may ask? Why not join another church? And I confess that if all that I knew of Reverend Wright were the snippets of those sermons that have run in an endless loop on the television and YouTube, or if Trinity United Church of Christ conformed to the caricatures being peddled by some commentators, there is no doubt that I would react in much the same way.

But the truth is, that isn't all that I know of the man. The man I met more than twenty years ago is a man who helped introduce me to my Christian faith, a man who spoke to me about our obligations to love one another; to care for the sick and lift up the poor. He is a man who served his country as a U.S. Marine; who has studied and lectured at some of the finest universities and seminaries in the country, and who for over thirty years led a church that serves the community by doing God's work here on Earth—by housing the homeless, ministering to the needy, providing day care services and scholarships and prison ministries, and reaching out to those suffering from HIV/AIDS.

In my first book, *Dreams from My Father,* I described the experience of my first service at Trinity:

> People began to shout, to rise from their seats and clap and cry out, a forceful wind carrying the reverend's voice up into the rafters. . . . And in that single note—hope!—I heard something else; at the foot of that cross, inside the thousands of churches across the city, I imagined the stories of ordinary black people merging with the stories of David and Goliath, Moses and Pharaoh, the Christians in the lion's den, Ezekiel's field of dry bones. Those stories—of survival, and freedom, and hope—became our story, my story; the blood that had spilled was our blood, the tears our tears; until this black church, on this bright day, seemed once more a vessel carrying the story of a people into future generations and into a larger world. Our trials and triumphs became at once unique and universal, black and more than black; in chronicling our journey, the stories and songs gave us a means to reclaim memories that we didn't need to feel

shame about . . . memories that all people might study and cherish—and with which we could start to rebuild.

That has been my experience at Trinity. Like other predominantly black churches across the country, Trinity embodies the black community in its entirety—the doctor and the welfare mom, the model student and the former gang-banger. Like other black churches, Trinity's services are full of raucous laughter and sometimes bawdy humor. They are full of dancing, clapping, screaming, and shouting that may seem jarring to the untrained ear. The church contains in full the kindness and cruelty, the fierce intelligence and the shocking ignorance, the struggles and successes, the love and, yes, the bitterness and bias that make up the black experience in America.

And this helps explain, perhaps, my relationship with Reverend Wright. As imperfect as he may be, he has been like family to me. He strengthened my faith, officiated my wedding, and baptized my children. Not once in my conversations with him have I heard him talk about any ethnic group in derogatory terms, or treat whites with whom he interacted with anything but courtesy and respect. He contains within him the contradictions—the good and the bad—of the community that he has served diligently for so many years.

I can no more disown him than I can disown the black community. I can no more disown him than I can my white grandmother—a woman who helped raise me, a woman who sacrificed again and again for me, a woman who loves me as much as she loves anything in this world, but a woman who once confessed her fear of black men who passed by her on the street, and who on more than one occasion has uttered racial or ethnic stereotypes that made me cringe.

These people are a part of me. And they are a part of America, this country that I love.

Some will see this as an attempt to justify or excuse comments that are simply inexcusable. I can assure you it is not.

I suppose the politically safe thing would be to move on from this episode and just hope that it fades into the woodwork. We can dismiss Reverend Wright as a crank or a demagogue, just as some have dismissed Geraldine Ferraro, in the aftermath of her recent statements, as harboring some deep-seated racial bias.

But race is an issue that I believe this nation cannot afford to ignore right now. We would be making the same mistake that Reverend Wright made in his offending sermons about America—to simplify and stereotype and amplify the negative to the point that it distorts reality.

The fact is that the comments that have been made and the issues that have surfaced over the last few weeks reflect the complexities of race in this country that we've never really worked through—a part of our union that we have yet to perfect. And if we walk away now, if we simply retreat into our respective corners, we will never be able to come together and solve challenges like health care, or education, or the need to find good jobs for every American.

Understanding this reality requires a reminder of how we arrived at this point. As William Faulkner once wrote, "The past isn't dead and buried. In fact, it isn't even past." We do not need to recite here the history of racial injustice in this country. But we do need to remind ourselves that so many of the disparities that exist in the African American community today can be directly traced to inequalities passed on from an earlier generation that suffered under the brutal legacy of slavery and Jim Crow.

Segregated schools were, and are, inferior schools; we still haven't fixed them, fifty years after *Brown v. Board of Education*, and the inferior education they provided, then and now, helps explain the pervasive achievement gap between today's black and white students.

Legalized discrimination—where blacks were prevented, often through violence, from owning property, or loans were not granted to African American business owners, or black homeowners could not access FHA mortgages, or blacks were excluded from unions, or the police force, or fire departments—meant that black families could not amass any meaningful wealth to bequeath to future generations. That history helps explain the wealth and income gap between black and white, and the concentrated pockets of poverty that persists in so many of today's urban and rural communities.

A lack of economic opportunity among black men, and the shame and frustration that came from not being able to provide for one's family, contributed to the erosion of black families—a problem that welfare policies for many years may have worsened. And the lack of basic services in so many urban black neighborhoods—parks for kids to play in, police walking the beat, regular garbage pick-up and building code enforcement—all helped create a cycle of violence, blight, and neglect that continue to haunt us.

This is the reality in which Reverend Wright and other African Americans of his generation grew up. They came of age in the late fifties and early sixties, a time when segregation was still the law of the land and opportunity was systematically constricted. What's remarkable is not how many failed in the face of discrimination, but rather how many men and women overcame the odds; how many were able to make a way out of no way for those like me who would come after them.

But for all those who scratched and clawed their way to get a piece of the American Dream, there were many who didn't make it—those who were ultimately defeated, in one way or another, by discrimination. That legacy of defeat was passed on to future generations—those young men and increasingly young women who we see standing on street corners or languishing in our prisons, without hope or prospects for the future. Even for those blacks who did make it, questions of race, and racism, continue to define their worldview in fundamental ways. For the men and women of Reverend Wright's generation, the memories of humiliation and doubt and fear have not gone away; nor has the anger and the bitterness of those years. That anger may not get expressed in public, in front of white coworkers or white friends. But it does find voice in the barbershop or around the kitchen table. At times, that anger is exploited by politicians, to gin up votes along racial lines, or to make up for a politician's own failings.

And occasionally it finds voice in the church on Sunday morning, in the pulpit and in the pews. The fact that so many people are surprised to hear that anger in some of Reverend Wright's sermons simply reminds us of the old truism that the most segregated hour in American life occurs on Sunday morning. That anger is not always productive; indeed, all too often it distracts attention from solving real problems; it keeps us from squarely facing our own complicity in our condition, and prevents the African American community from forging the alliances it needs to bring about real change. But the anger is real; it is powerful; and to simply wish it away, to condemn it without understanding its roots, only serves to widen the chasm of misunderstanding that exists between the races.

In fact, a similar anger exists within segments of the white community. Most working- and middle-class white Americans don't feel that they have been particularly privileged by their race. Their experience is the immigrant experience—as far as they're concerned, no one's handed them anything, they've built it from scratch. They've worked hard all their lives, many times only to see their jobs shipped overseas or their pension dumped after a lifetime of labor. They are anxious about their futures, and feel their dreams slipping away; in an era of stagnant wages and global competition, opportunity comes to be seen as a zero sum game, in which your dreams come at my expense. So when they are told to bus their children to a school across town; when they hear that an African American is getting an advantage in landing a good job or a spot in a good college because of an injustice that they themselves never committed; when they're told that their fears about crime in urban neighborhoods are somehow prejudiced, resentment builds over time.

Like the anger within the black community, these resentments aren't always expressed in polite company. But they have helped shape the political landscape for at least a generation. Anger over welfare and affirmative action helped forge the Reagan Coalition. Politicians routinely exploited fears of crime for their own electoral ends. Talk show hosts and conservative commentators built entire careers unmasking bogus claims of racism while dismissing legitimate discussions of racial injustice and inequality as mere political correctness or reverse racism.

Just as black anger often proved counterproductive, so have these white resentments distracted attention from the real culprits of the middle-class squeeze—a corporate culture rife with inside dealing, questionable accounting practices, and short-term greed; a Washington dominated by lobbyists and special interests; economic policies that favor the few over the many. And yet, to wish away the resentments of white Americans, to label them as misguided or even racist, without recognizing they are grounded in legitimate concerns—this too widens the racial divide, and blocks the path to understanding.

This is where we are right now. It's a racial stalemate we've been stuck in for years. Contrary to the claims of some of my critics, black and white, I have never been so naïve as to believe that we can get beyond our racial divisions in a single election cycle, or with a single candidacy—particularly a candidacy as imperfect as my own.

But I have asserted a firm conviction—a conviction rooted in my faith in God and my faith in the American people—that working together we can move beyond some of our old racial wounds, and that in fact we have no choice if we are to continue on the path of a more perfect union.

For the African American community, that path means embracing the burdens of our past without becoming victims of our past. It means continuing to insist on a full measure of justice in every aspect of American life. But it also means binding our particular grievances—for better health care, and better schools, and better jobs—to the larger aspirations of all Americans—the white woman struggling to break the glass ceiling, the white man who's been laid off, the immigrant trying to feed his family. And it means taking full responsibility for our own lives—by demanding more from our fathers, and spending more time with our children, and reading to them, and teaching them that while they may face challenges and discrimination in their own lives, they must never succumb to despair or cynicism; they must always believe that they can write their own destiny.

Ironically, this quintessentially American—and, yes, conservative—notion of self-help found frequent expression in Reverend Wright's sermons. But what my former pastor too often failed to understand is that embarking on a program of self-help also requires a belief that society can change.

The profound mistake of Reverend Wright's sermons is not that he spoke about racism in our society. It's that he spoke as if our society was static; as if no progress has been made; as if this country—a country that has made it possible for one of his own members to run for the highest office in the land and build a coalition of white and black, Latino and Asian, rich and poor, young and old—is still irrevocably bound to a tragic past. But what we know—what we have seen—is that America can change. That is the true genius of this nation. What we have already achieved gives us hope—the audacity to hope—for what we can and must achieve tomorrow.

In the white community, the path to a more perfect union means acknowledging that what ails the African American community does not just exist in the minds of black people; that the legacy of discrimination—and current incidents of discrimination, while less overt than in the past—are real and must be addressed. Not just with words, but with deeds—by investing in our schools and our communities; by enforcing our civil rights laws and ensuring fairness in our criminal justice system; by providing this generation with ladders of opportunity that were unavailable for previous generations. It requires all Americans to realize that your dreams do not have to come at the expense of my dreams; that investing in the health, welfare, and education of black and brown and white children will ultimately help all of America prosper.

In the end, then, what is called for is nothing more, and nothing less, than what all the world's great religions demand—that we do unto others as we would have them do unto us. Let us be our brother's keeper, Scripture tells us. Let us be our sister's keeper. Let us find that common stake we all have in one another, and let our politics reflect that spirit as well.

For we have a choice in this country. We can accept a politics that breeds division, and conflict, and cynicism. We can tackle race only as spectacle—as we did in the OJ trial—or in the wake of tragedy, as we did in the aftermath of Katrina—or as fodder for the nightly news. We can play Reverend Wright's sermons on every channel, every day and talk about them from now until the election, and make the only question in this campaign whether or not the American people think that I somehow believe or sympathize with his most offensive words. We can pounce on some gaffe by a Hillary supporter as evidence that she's playing the race card, or we can speculate on whether white men will all flock to John McCain in the general election regardless of his policies.

We can do that.

But if we do, I can tell you that in the next election, we'll be talking about some other distraction. And then another one. And then another one. And nothing will change.

That is one option. Or, at this moment, in this election, we can come together and say, "Not this time." This time we want to talk about the crumbling schools that are stealing the future of black children and white children and Asian children and Hispanic children and Native American children. This time we want to reject the cynicism that tells us that these kids can't learn; that those kids who don't look like us are somebody else's problem. The children of America are not those kids, they are our kids, and we will not let them fall behind in a twenty-first-century economy. Not this time.

This time we want to talk about how the lines in the emergency room are filled with whites and blacks and Hispanics who do not have health care; who don't have the power on their own to overcome the special interests in Washington, but who can take them on if we do it together.

This time we want to talk about the shuttered mills that once provided a decent life for men and women of every race, and the homes for sale that once belonged to Americans from every religion, every region, every walk of life. This time we want to talk about the fact that the real problem is not that someone who doesn't look like you might take your job; it's that the corporation you work for will ship it overseas for nothing more than a profit.

This time we want to talk about the men and women of every color and creed who serve together, and fight together, and bleed together under the same proud flag. We want to talk about how to bring them home from a war that never should've been authorized and never should've been waged, and we want to talk about how we'll show our patriotism by caring for them, and their families, and giving them the benefits they have earned.

I would not be running for president if I didn't believe with all my heart that this is what the vast majority of Americans want for this country. This union may never be perfect, but generation after generation has shown that it can always be perfected. And today, whenever I find myself feeling doubtful or cynical about this possibility, what gives me the most hope is the next generation—the young people whose attitudes and beliefs and openness to change have already made history in this election.

There is one story in particularly that I'd like to leave you with today—a story I told when I had the great honor of speaking on Dr. King's birthday at his home church, Ebenezer Baptist, in Atlanta.

There is a young twenty-three-year-old white woman named Ashley Baia who organized for our campaign in Florence, South Carolina. She had been working to organize a mostly African American community since the beginning of this campaign, and one day she was at a roundtable discussion where everyone went around telling their story and why they were there.

And Ashley said that when she was nine years old, her mother got cancer. And because she had to miss days of work, she was let go and lost her health care. They had to file for bankruptcy, and that's when Ashley decided that she had to do something to help her mom.

She knew that food was one of their most expensive costs, and so Ashley convinced her mother that what she really liked and really wanted to eat more than anything else was mustard and relish sandwiches. Because that was the cheapest way to eat.

She did this for a year until her mom got better, and she told everyone at the roundtable that the reason she joined our campaign was so that she could help the millions of other children in the country who want and need to help their parents too.

Now Ashley might have made a different choice. Perhaps somebody told her along the way that the source of her mother's problems were blacks who were on welfare and too lazy to work, or Hispanics who were coming into the country illegally. But she didn't. She sought out allies in her fight against injustice.

Anyway, Ashley finishes her story and then goes around the room and asks everyone else why they're supporting the campaign. They all have different stories and reasons. Many bring up a specific issue. And finally they come to this elderly black man who's been sitting there quietly the entire time. And Ashley asks him why he's there. And he does not bring up a specific issue. He does not say health care or the economy. He does not say education or the war. He does not say that he was there because of Barack Obama. He simply says to everyone in the room, "I am here because of Ashley."

"I'm here because of Ashley." By itself, that single moment of recognition between that young white girl and that old black man is not enough. It is not enough to give health care to the sick, or jobs to the jobless, or education to our children.

But it is where we start. It is where our union grows stronger. And as so many generations have come to realize over the course of the two hundred and twenty-one years since a band of patriots signed that document in Philadelphia, that is where the perfection begins.

Notes

Introduction

1. Kevin Sacks, "A Time to Reap for Foot Soldiers of Civil Rights," *New York Times*, November 4, 2008 (hereafter *NYT*).

2. A process that Obama began with his keynote address at the 2004 Democratic National Convention (see David Mendell, *Obama: From Promise to Power* [New York: Amistad Press, 2007], 3).

3. Abby Goodnough, "Massachusetts Votes to Keep Its Income Tax," *NYT*, November 5, 2008.

4. Many of the Republican Party's voter base demonstrated the importance of issues like gender and sexuality after Senator John McCain announced his vice-presidential running mate was Alaska governor Sarah Palin. Much of the initial response from Republican voters was openly chauvinistic; the following comment of one correspondent to the *Houston Chronicle* was typical: "Other than a pretty face, what is Gov. Sarah Palin going to bring to the Republican ticket?" (August 30, 2008). For scholarly analysis of race, sexuality, and gender in the United States, see John D'Emilio and Estelle B. Freedman, *Intimate Matters: A History of Sexuality in America* (Chicago: University of Chicago Press, 1997); Julian B. Carter, *The Heart of Whiteness: Normal Sexuality and Race in America, 1880–1940* (Durham: Duke University Press, 2007); Mary K. Bloodsworth-Lugo, *In-Between Bodies: Sexual Difference, Race,*

and Sexuality (Albany: SUNY Press, 2007); and Jared Sexton, *Amalgamation Schemes: Antiblackness and the Critique of Multiculturalism* (Minneapolis: University of Minnesota Press, 2008).

5. Quoted in Martin Fletcher and James Bone, "Hugs and High Fives as a Spirit of Harmony Blows into Windy City," *Times* (London), November 6, 2008.

6. http://www.conservapedia.com/Barack_Obama.

7. Sarah Smith, "Police Foil Plot to Kill Obama," *Channel 4 News*, http://www.channel4.com/news/articles/politics/international_politics/police+foil+plot+to+kill+obama/2673987; Jonah Goldberg, "'Hear Me, Earthlings!' Citizen Obama Addresses the World," *National Review*, August 18, 2008, 18; David van Drehle, "The Five Faces of Barack Obama," *Time*, September 1, 2008, 33; David Freddoso, *The Case against Barack Obama: The Unlikely Rise and Unexamined Agenda of the Media's Favorite Candidate* (Washington, D.C.: Regnery, 2008), 121. For a brief summation of Obama conspiracy theories, see "Explaining the Riddle," *Economist*, August 23–29, 2008, 20.

8. Bruce R. Dain, *A Hideous Monster of the Mind: American Race Theory in the Early Republic* (Cambridge: Harvard University Press, 2002); George M. Fredrickson, *Racism: A Short History* (Princeton: Princeton University Press, 2002); Gary Gerstle, *American Crucible: Race and Nation in the Twentieth Century* (Princeton: Princeton University Press, 2002); Jerrold M. Packard, *American Nightmare: The History of Jim Crow* (New York: St. Martin's Press, 2002); John M. Giggie, *After Redemption: Jim Crow and the Transformation of African American Religion in the Delta, 1875–1915* (New York: Oxford University Press, 2007); Clive Webb, *Massive Resistance: Southern Opposition to the Second Reconstruction* (New York: Oxford University Press, 2005); George Lewis, *Massive Resistance: The White Response to the Civil Rights Movement* (London: Hodder Arnold, 2006).

9. http://www.shitskin.com/presidentshitskin.html.

10. Jay Felsberg, "Board Won't Fire Teacher over Obama Slur," *Florida Freedom Newspaper*, October 17, 2008, http://www.nwfdailynews.com/news/howard_11960_article.html/board_sims.html.

11. Sarah Smith, "Police Foil Plot to Kill Obama."

12. See *TV by the Numbers*, http://tvbythenumbers.com/2009/01/

16/oreilly-vs-olbermann-through-thursday-january-15/11035#more-11035.

13. Bruce A. Williams and Michelle X. Delli Carpini, "The Eroding Boundaries between News and Entertainment and What They Mean for Democratic Politics," in *The Handbook of Mass Media Ethics*, ed. Lee Wilkins and Clifford G. Christians (New York and London: Taylor and Frances, 2008), 181. See also Stephen J. Farnsworth and S. Robert Lichter, *The Nightly News Nightmare: Television's Coverage of U.S. Presidential Elections, 1988–2004* (New York: Rowan and Littlefield, 2007).

14. See *NationMaster*, http://www.nationmaster.com/encyclopedia/PBS-Newshour; Robert J. McKeever and Philip Davies, *Introduction to US Politics* (New York: Pearson Longman), 82. For further analysis, see James T. Hamilton, *All the News That's Fit to Sell: How the Market Transforms Information into News* (Princeton: Princeton University Press, 2006); Mark J. Rozell and Jeremy D. Mayer, *Media Power, Media Politics*, 2nd ed. (New York: Rowan and Littlefield, 2008).

15. Greg Hitt, "The New Southern Strategy," *Wall Street Journal*, August 7, 2008; Christopher Dickey, "Southern Discomfort," *Newsweek*, August 11, 2008, 22–32.

16. C. Vann Woodward, *Origins of the New South, 1877–1913* (Baton Rouge: Louisiana State University Press, 1971); Edward L. Ayers, *The Promise of the New South: Life after Reconstruction* (1992; New York: Oxford University Press, 2007), 272, 413; Holland Thompson, *The New South: A Chronicle of Social and Industrial Evolution* (Charleston: BiblioBazaar, 2008), 53.

17. Ayers, *The Promise of the New South*, 18; Stephen D. Shaffer, Charles E. Menifield, Peter W. Wielhouwer, and Keesha M. Middlemass, "An Introduction to Southern Legislative Coalitions," in *Politics in the New South: Representations of African Americans in Southern State Legislatures*, ed. Menifield and Shaffer (Albany: SUNY Press, 2005), 17.

18. Hitt, "The New Southern Strategy."

19. Jack Bass, "In Dixie, Signs of a Rising Biracial Politics," *NYT*, May 11, 2008.

20. Jason Horowitz, "Black Congressmen Declare Racism in Palin's Rhetoric," *New York Observer*, October 7, 2008, http://www.observer.com/2008/politics/black-congressmen-declare-racism-palin-s-rhetoric.

21. Obama, *Dreams from My Father: A Story of Race and Inheritance* (1995; New York: Three Rivers Press, 2004), v.

22. Kate Phillips, "Palin: Obama Is 'Palling around with Terrorists,'" *Caucus, NYT* political blog, October 4, 2008, http://thecaucus.blogs.nytimes.com/2008/10/04/palin-obama-is-palling-around-with-terrorists/; Cliff Kincaid, "Is Barack Obama a Secret Marxist Mole?" *Canada Free Press,* March 19, 2008, http://www.canadafreepress.com/index.php/article/2289. Ann Coulter's article about Obama's memoir inspired one reader to write, "For the first time in my adult life, I'm really proud to be a . . . typical white person" (see Ann Coulter, "Obama's Dimestore *Mein Kampf,*" *Human Events,* April 2, 2008, http://www.humanevents.com/article.php?id=25831&keywords=dimestore+mein+kampf).

23. For a sampling of opinions that emphasized "not really knowing Obama," see Jack Kelly, "Obama's Fishy Associations: Still No Answers to Questions on Ayers and Others," *Pittsburgh Post-Gazette,* October 12, 2008, http://www.post-gazette.com/pg/08286/919158-373.stm; and Frank Diamond, "We Don't Really Know Obama," *Bulletin: Philadelphia's Family Newspaper,* October 22, 2008, http://www.thebulletin.us. For Obama's lack of experience, see Judy Keen, "The Big Question about Barack Obama," *USA Today,* January 17, 2007, http://www.usatoday.com/news/washington/2007-01-16-obama-experience-cover_x.htm; "Obama Lacks Experience to Be Next President," Letters to the Editor, *Delaware Online,* October 8, 2008, http://www.delawareonline.com/; Evelyn O. Hassell, "Obama Lacks Needed Experience for Office," *Shreveport Times,* October 31, 2008, http://www.shreveporttimes.com/. For Obama's "split personality," see David Brooks, "The Two Obamas," *NYT,* June 20, 2008.

24. Obama has himself made comments that many interpret as "postracial." For example, he claimed in 1995 that the "world will [eventually] look more like Brazil, with its racial mix. America is getting more complex. The color line in America being black and white is out the window. That does break down barriers" (Lisa Rogak, ed., *Barack Obama: In His Own Words* [New York: Carroll and Graf, 2007], 94).

25. Suki Ali, *Mixed-Race, Post-Race: Gender, New Ethnicities and Cultural Practices* (Oxford: Berg, 2003), 2, 9.

26. See http://www.youtube.com/watch?v=ISOBxlHuosE.

27. Poll data collected during the presidential election campaign suggested that racial considerations still weighed heavily on the minds of American voters. In one study, for example, 59 percent of African Americans, compared with only 34 percent of whites, considered race relations to be bad, results that testify to the divergent racial perceptions that remain in the United States (Adam Nagourney and Megan Thee, "Poll Finds Obama Isn't Closing Divide on Race," *NYT*, July 16, 2008, http://www.nytimes.com/2008/07/16/us/politics/16poll.html?=5070&en=f98d57e0c51fe). See also Peter J. Boyer, "The Color of Politics: A Mayor of the Post-Racial Generation," *New Yorker*, February 4, 2008, 38–51.

28. Andrew Rawnsley, "Obama Needs Americans to Believe He Is One of Them," *Guardian* (Manchester), August 24, 2008, http://www.guardian.co.uk/commentisfree/2008/aug/24/barackobama.democrats 2008.

29. We refer in particular to headlines such as "History in the Making," *Jet*, January 21, 2008, 6. Books that address issues of race and Obama's candidacy range from superficial philosophical musings by Shelby Steele, to party-political volumes by authors such as Jerome Corsi and David Freddoso that lack any scholarly merit (see Shelby Steele, *A Bound Man: Why We Are Excited about Obama and Why He Can't Win* [New York: Free Press, 2007]; Jerome R. Corsi, *The Obama Nation: Leftist Politics and the Cult of Personality* [New York: Threshold Editions, 2008]; and David Freddoso, *The Case against Barack Obama: The Unlikely Rise and Unexamined Agenda of the Media's Favorite Candidate* [Washington, D.C.: Regnery, 2008]).

30. See, for example, Kevin Chappell, "Barack Obama Answers Critics; Delivers Historic Speech on Race in America," *Jet*, April 7, 2008, 10–14; Lisa Miller and Richard Wolffe, "Finding His Faith," *Newsweek*, July 21, 2008, 27–32; and Peter J. Boyer, "Party Faithful: Can the Democrats Get a Foothold on the Religious Vote?" *New Yorker*, September 8, 2008, 24–31.

31. Stephen Mansfield, *The Faith of Barack Obama* (Nashville: Thomas Nelson, 2008), 134.

32. One *New York Times* blog received over nine hundred responses, ranging from the outraged to the sympathetic (see http://thecaucus

.blogs.nytimes.com/2008/04/28/rev-wright-defends-church-blasts-media/?scp=2-b&sq=rev.+wright&st=nyt).

33. Nathan Irvin Huggins, *Revelations: American History, American Myths* (New York: Oxford University Press, 1995), 253.

34. Dwight N. Hopkins, *Heart and Head: Black Theology—Past, Present, and Future* (New York: Palgrave-Macmillan, 2002), 29.

35. David J. Bederman, *The Classical Foundations of the American Constitution: Prevailing Wisdom* (Cambridge: Cambridge University Press, 2008), 102

36. Huggins, *Revelations*, 279.

1. The "Chickens Are Coming Home to Roost"

1. http://www.youtube.com/watch?v=36TfafCo.

2. Ibid.

3. Shulamit Volkov, *Germans, Jews, and Antisemites* (Cambridge: Cambridge University Press, 2006), 163. See also Michael Marrus, *The Politics of Assimilation: The French Jewish Community at the Time of the Dreyfus Affair* (Oxford: Oxford University Press, 1981); Susan E. Shapiro, "*Ecriture judaique:* Where are the Jews in Western Discourse?" in *Displacements: Cultural Identities in Question*, ed. Angelika Bammer (Bloomington: Indiana University Press, 1994), 194.

4. Volkov, *Germans, Jews, and Antisemites*, 162.

5. See Clarence E. Walker, *A Rock in a Weary Land: The African Methodist Episcopal Church during the Civil War and Reconstruction* (Baton Rouge: Louisiana University Press, 1982).

6. See, for example, Elisha Bates, *The Doctrine of Friends: Or, the Principle of the Christian Religion, as Held by the Society of Friends, Commonly Called Quakers* (Mount Pleasant, Ohio, 1829), 14. See also Manning Marable, *Black Liberation in Conservative America* (Boston: South End Press, 1997), 74; and J. Deotis Roberts, *Bonhoeffer and King: Speaking Truth to Power* (Louisville: Westminster John Knox Press, 2005), 6.

7. "A Model of Christian Charity," by Governor John Winthrop, 1630, http://religiousfreedom.lib.Virginia.edu/.

8. *The Holy Bible, King James Version* (New York: New American Library, 1974), 646.

9. Quoted in Bernard Bailyn, *The Ideological Origins of the American*

Revolution (New York: Belknap Press of Harvard University Press, 1967), 233.

10. Quoted in Peter Hinks, *To Awaken My Afflicted Brethren: David Walker and the Problem of Antebellum Slave Resistance* (University Park: Pennsylvania State University Press, 1997), 175.

11. Ibid., 176

12. Rt. Rev. Richard Allen, *The Life Experience and Gospel Labors of the Rt. Rev Richard Allen: To Which Is Annexed the Rise and Progress of the African Methodist Episcopal Church in the United States of America: Containing a Narrative of the Yellow Fever in the Year of Our Lord, 1793: With an Address to the People of Color in the United States* (1794; repr., Nashville: Abingdon Press, 1983), 69–70.

13. Hinks, *To Awaken My Afflicted Brethren*, 173.

14. Peter Hinks, ed., *David Walker's Appeal to the Coloured Citizens of the World* (1829; repr., University Park: Pennsylvania State University Press, 2000), 79.

15. David Howard-Pitney, *The African American Jeremiad: Appeals for Justice in America* (Philadelphia: Temple University Press, 2005), 18.

16. Christopher B. Booker, *"I Will Wear No Chain": A Social History of African American Males* (Westport, Conn: Greenwood, 2008), 68.

17. Eugene Genovese, *A Consuming Fire: The Fall of the Confederacy in the Mind of the White Christian South* (Athens: University of Georgia Press, 1998), 101.

18. Daniel Stowell, *Rebuilding Zion: The Religious Reconstruction of the South, 1863–1877* (New York: Oxford University Press, 1998), 37. See also Ann S. Rubin, *A Shattered Nation: The Rise and Fall of the Confederacy, 1861–1868* (Chapel Hill: University of North Carolina Press, 2005), 64.

19. Howard-Pitney, *The African American Jeremiad*, 10.

20. Quoted in Walker, *A Rock in a Weary Land*, 35.

21. *Lincoln: Speeches, Letters, Miscellaneous Writings, Presidential Messages and Proclamations* (New York: Library of America, 1973), 687.

22. George R. Price and James Brewer Stewart, eds., *To Heal the Scourge of Prejudice: The Life and Writings of Hosea Easton* (Amherst: University of Massachusetts Press, 1999), 106; Gilbert Osofsky, *The Burden of Race: A Documentary History of Negro White Relations in America*

(New York: Harper and Row, 1967), 69; Paul Goodman, *Of One Blood: Abolitionism and the Origins of Racial Equality* (Berkeley and Los Angeles: University of California Press, 1998), 30.

23. Quoted in Leon F. Litwack, *Been in the Storm So Long* (New York: Knopf, 1979), 464.

24. Ibid.

25. Quoted in Lawrence W. Levine, *Black Culture and Black Consciousness* (New York: Oxford University Press, 1977), 33.

26. E. Franklin Frazier, *The Negro Church in America* (New York: Schocken Books, 1964), 16–19.

27. Howard-Pitney, *The African American Jeremiad*, 11–12.

28. C. Eric Lincoln and Lawrence H. Mamiya, *The Black Church in the African American Experience* (Durham: Duke University Press, 1990), 8–9.

29. Benjamin Quarles, *Black Abolitionists* (1969; repr., New York: Da Capo Press, 1991), 28.

30. For the American Colonization Society's goals, see Fredrickson, *The Black Image in the White Mind*, chap. 1. See also Emma Jones Lapansky, "'Since They Got Those Separate Churches': Afro-Americans and Racism in Jacksonian Philadelphia," in *African-American Activism before the Civil War*, ed. Patrick Rael (New York: Routledge, 2008), 114.

31. Quoted in Lapansky, "Since They Got Those Separate Churches," 105.

32. Ralph David Abernathy, *And the Walls Came Tumbling Down: An Autobiography* (New York: Harper and Row, 1989), 296.

33. Details of Wright's life can be found in Jeremiah A. Wright, *The Pilgrimage of a Pastor: The Autobiography of Jeremiah A. Wright, Sr.* (Morristown, N.J.: Aaron Press, 1989); and Emily Udell, "Keeping the Faith," *In These Times*, February 8, 2005.

34. Hopkins, *Heart and Head*, 14.

35. See the reader comments posted to Jeff Zeleny, "Obama Voters Don't Want Drama," *Caucus*, *NYT* political blog, May 2, 2008, http://thecaucus.blogs.nytimes.com/2008/05/02/obama-voters-dont-want-drama/?scp=1&sq=%22Obama%20Voters%20Don't%20Want%20Drama%22&st=cse.

36. See Sacvan Bercovitch, *The American Jeremiad* (Madison: Uni-

versity of Wisconsin Press, 1978); Howard-Pitney, *The African American Jeremiad.*

37. As one writer on the Web site *Black Commentator* noted of the traditional narrative of American history: "The settlers were heroes; the indigenous people were either heathens or native primitives, but in either case they were in the way of progress. Slavery was an unfortunate episode that was cleaned up by the Civil War, though it has never been clear that the former slaves were ever meant to rule themselves, let alone anyone else. U.S. foreign policy has generally been benign, nearly always driven by either God-given imperative to improve the world or our sense that the world would be better off with our version of capitalism and democracy" (http://www.blackcommentator.com/276/276/_think_aw_icarus_obama).

38. "The Full Story behind Rev. Jeremiah Wright's 9/11 Sermon," March 21, 2008, http://ac360.blogs.cnn.com/2008/03/21/the-full-story-behind-rev-jeremiah-wrights-911-sermon/.

39. Ibid.

40. Quoted in David Remnick, "The Joshua Generation," *New Yorker,* November, 17, 2008, 81–82.

41. Bill Freind, "Post Modern Eden: Nature and the City on a Hill in Charles Olson's The Maximus Poems," in *From Virgin Land to Disney World: Nature and Its Discontents in the USA of Yesterday and Today,* ed. Bernd Herzogenrath (Amsterdam: Rodopi, 2001), 130.

42. For this process, see J. H. Elliot, *Empires of the Atlantic World: Britain and Spain in America 1492–1830* (New Haven: Yale University Press, 2006); Norbert Finzch, "'The Aborigines . . . Were Never Annihilated, and Still They Are Becoming Extinct': Settler Imperialism and Genocide in Nineteenth-Century America and Australia" in *Empire, Colony, Genocide, Conquest, Occupation and Subaltern Resistance in World History,* ed. A. Dirk Moses (New York: Berghahn Books 2008), 253–70; Ben Kiernan, *Blood and Soil: A World History of Genocide and Extermination from Sparta to Darfur* (New Haven: Yale University Press, 2007); Alan Taylor, *American Colonies* (New York: Viking, 2001); and Patrick Wolf, "Land, Labor, and Difference: Elementary Structures of Race," *American Historical Review* 106, no. 3 (June 2001): 866–905.

43. Obama, *Dreams from My Father,* 203.

44. See, for example, Saul S. Friedman, *A History of the Holocaust* (London: Vallentine Mitchell, 2004); Donald Bloxham, *The Great Game of Genocide: Imperialism, Nationalism, and the Destruction of the Ottoman Armenians* (Oxford: Oxford University Press, 2005).

45. Harriet A. Washington, *Medical Apartheid: The Dark History of Medical Experimentation on Black Americans from Colonial Times to the Present* (New York: Doubleday, 2006), 59–61.

46. F. N. Boney, ed., *Slave Life in Georgia: A Narrative of the Life, Suffering & Escape of John Brown* (1855; repr., Savannah: Beehive Press, 1972), 41–43.

47. J. Marion Simms, "Two Cases of Vesico-Vaginal Fistula, Cured," *New York Medical Gazette* 5, no. 1 (1854): 1–7. See also Deborah Khun McGregor, *From Midwives to Medicine: The Birth of American Gynecology* (Newark: Rutgers University Press, 1998), chap. 2; Washington, *Medical Apartheid*, 61–65.

48. James H. Jones, *Bad Blood: The Tuskegee Syphilis Experiment* (New York: Free Press, 1981).

49. Washington, *Medical Apartheid*, 203–4.

50. Michael Powell and Jodi Kantor, "After Attacks, Michelle Obama Looks for a New Introduction," *NYT*, June 18, 2008, http://www.nytimes.com/.

51. Jeremiah A. Wright, *What Makes You So Strong?: Sermons of Joy and Strength from Jeremiah A. Wright, Jr.*, ed. Jini Kilgore Ross (Valley Forge, Pa.: Judson Press, 1993), 134.

52. Angela D. Dillard, "Religion and Radicalism: The Reverend Albert B. Cleage, Jr., and the Rise of Black Christian Nationalism in Detroit," in *Freedom North: Black Freedom Struggles Outside the South, 1940–1980*, ed. Jeanne F. Theoharis and Komozi Woodard (New York: Palgrave-Macmillan, 2003), 158.

53. Jodi Kantor, "Obama Quits His Church after Pastor Controversy," *NYT*, June 1, 2008.

54. Hopkins, *Heart and Head*, 53–54.

55. Milmon F. Harrison, *Righteous Riches: The Word of Faith Movement in Contemporary African American Religion* (New York: Oxford University Press, 2005). See the introduction and back cover of this work for an explanation of this movement. See also Kelefa Sanneh, "Pray and Grow Rich: Dr. Creflo Dollar's Ministry of Money," *New Yorker*, October

11, 2004, 48–57; and John F. MacArthur, *Charismatic Chaos* (Grand Rapids: Zondervan, 1993), 323. For the origins of this movement, see Donald Myers's magisterial *The Positive Thinkers: Religion as Pop Psychology, from Mary Baker Eddy to Oral Roberts* (New York: Pantheon Books, 1965).

56. For "mind cure," see Myers, *The Positive Thinkers*, chap. 2.

57. Alan Taylor, "The Old Frontiers," *New Republic*, May 27, 2008, 53.

58. Mark A. Knoll, *The Scandal of the Evangelical Mind* (Grand Rapids: Eerdmans, 1994), 4.

59. It is our contention that the quest for a Christianity that ministers to the particular needs of black people did not begin in 1969, when the Reverend James Cone published his influential *Black Theology and Black Power*, but must be dated to a much earlier period.

60. For the emergence of these denominations, see Carol George, *Segregated Sabbaths: Richard Allen and the Rise of Independent Black Churches, 1760–1840* (New York: Oxford University Press, 1973); Lincoln and Mamiya, *The Black Church in the African American Experience*; and Walker, *A Rock in a Weary Land*.

61. Quoted in Litwack, *Trouble in Mind*, 392.

62. Quoted ibid., 393.

63. Ibid.

64. As a child attending black church services in California and Texas, Clarence Walker was exposed to the iconography of the black sanctuary.

65. For an example of this genre, see *King of Kings* (Metro-Goldwyn-Mayer, 1961). This movie starred the late Jeffrey Hunter. *The Last Temptation of Christ*, another film with an Aryan Christ, starred Willem Dafoe (Universal City Studios, 1988).

66. Wright, *What Makes You So Strong?* 147.

67. Gregory D. Smithers, "'Black Gentleman as Good as White': A Comparative Analysis of African American and Australian Aboriginal Political Protests, 1830–1865," *Journal of African American History* 93, no. 3 (Summer 2008): 320, 323.

68. See, for example, Molefi K. Asante, *Afrocentricity: The Theory of Social Change* (Trenton, N.J.: Africa World Press, 1998); Algernon Austin, *Achieving Blackness: Race, Black Nationalism and Afrocentrism in*

the Twentieth Century (New York: NYU Press, 2006); *The Autobiography of Malcolm X*, with Alex Haley (New York: Ballantine Books, 1964); Tommie Shelby, *We Who Are Dark: The Philosophical Foundations of Black Solidarity* (Cambridge: Harvard University Press, 2005); and E. U. Essien-Udom, *Black Nationalism: A Search for an Identity in America* (Chicago: University of Chicago Press, 1971).

69. George S. Schuyler, *Black No More: Being an Account of the Strange and Wonderful Workings of Science in the Land of the Free, A.D. 1933–1940* (New York: Macaulay Press, 1931).

70. *Bill Moyers Journal*, April 25, 2008, http://www.pbs.org/moyers/journal/04252008/transcript1.html.

71. Howard Winant, "Behind Blue Eyes: Whiteness and Contemporary U.S. Racial Politics," in *Off White: Readings on Power, Privilege, and Resistance*, ed. Michelle Fine, 2nd ed. (New York: Routledge, 2004), 9; David R. Roediger, *Colored White: Transcending the Racial Past* (Berkeley and Los Angeles: University of California Press, 2002), 58; Katharyne Mitchell, *Crossing the Neoliberal Line: Pacific Rim Migration and the Metropolis* (Philadelphia: Temple University Press, 2004), 10; Patricia Williams, *Seeing a Color-Blind Future* (New York: Noonday Press, 1997), passim; Howard Winant, *The New Politics of Race: From Du Bois to the 21st Century* (Minneapolis: Greenwood Publishing Group, 2004), passim.

72. Steele, *A Bound Man*, 4.

73. Audrey Smedley, *Race in North America: Origin and Evolution of a Worldview* (Boulder: Westview Press, 1993), 20.

74. Hazel Carby quoted in Richard Dyer, *White* (New York and London: Routledge, 1997), 3.

75. Winthrop D. Jordan, "American Chiaroscuro: The Status and Definition of Mulattoes in the British Colonies," *William and Mary Quarterly* (April 1962); Gregory D. Smithers, *Science, Sexuality, and Race in the United States and Australia, 1780s–1890s* (New York and London: Routledge, 2008); Clarence E. Walker, *Mongrel Nation: The America Begotten by Thomas Jefferson and Sally Hemings* (Charlottesville: University of Virginia Press, 2009).

76. George Fredrickson, *The Black Image in the White Mind: The Debate on Afro-American Character and Destiny, 1817–1914* (Middletown:

Wesleyan University Press, 1971), passim; John Hope Franklin and Alfred Moss, *From Slavery to Freedom: A History of Negro America*, 7th ed. (New York: Knopf, 1994), passim.

77. Manning Marable, *Living Black History: How Reimagining the African-American Past Can Remake America's Racial Future* (New York: Basic Civitas, 2006), 2.

78. Winant, *The New Politics of Race*, 55.

79. See also Jared Sexton, *Amalgamation Schemes: Antiblackness and the Critique of Multiculturalism* (Minneapolis: University of Minnesota Press, 2008), 65.

80. "The Big Remaining Question," *Economist*, May 10–16, 2008, 38.

81. Wright, *What Makes You So Strong?* 67.

82. James Baldwin, *Collected Essays* (New York: Library of America, 1998), 70.

83. Donald G. Baker, *Race, Ethnicity, and Power: A Comparative Study* (New York and London: Routledge, 1983); Jock Collins, *Confronting Racism in Australia, Canada, and New Zealand* (Sydney: University of Technology, 1995); Saul DeBow, *Scientific Racism in Modern South Africa* (Cambridge: Cambridge University Press, 1995).

84. Alan J. Singer, *New York and Slavery: Time to Teach the Truth* (Albany: SUNY Press, 2008), 1; Catherine Gunther Kodat, "Disney's *Song of the South* and the Birth of the White Negro," in *American Cold War Culture*, ed. Douglas Field (Edinburgh: Edinburgh University Press, 2005), 109–10.

85. Clayborne Carson, ed., *The Papers of Martin Luther King, Jr.. Threshold of a New Decade, January 1959–December 1960*, 6 vols. (Berkeley and Los Angeles: University of California Press, 1992–2006), 5:435.

86. *NYT*, November 2, 2008.

87. Ibid; Malcolm X, 301.

88. George Breitman, ed., *Malcolm X Speaks: Selected Speeches and Statements* (New York: Grove Weidenfeld, 1965), 26.

89. See, for example, William Julius Wilson, *The Declining Significance of Race: Blacks and Changing American Institutions* (Chicago: University of Chicago Press, 1980); Steven Hahn, *The Roots of Southern Populism: Yeoman Farmers and the Transformation of the Georgia Upcountry,*

1850–1890 (New York: Oxford University Press, 1983); Barbara J. Fields, "Ideology and Race in American History," in *Region, Race, and Reconstruction: Essays in Honor of C. Vann Woodward,* ed. J. Morgan Kousser and James McPherson (New York: Oxford University Press, 1982), 143–77; and "Slavery, Race and Ideology in the United States of America," *New Left Review,* 181 (1990): 95–118.

90. "Many Blacks Find Joy in Unexpected Breakthrough," *NYT,* June 5, 2008.

91. Martin Peretz, "Why Barack Obama Was Right Not to Repudiate His Pastor," *New Republic,* April 23, 2008, 15.

92. Valeria Sinclair-Chapman and Melanye Price, "Black Politics, the 2008 Election, and the (Im)Possibility of Race Transcendence," *PS: Political Science & Politics,* October 2008, 740.

93. "Wright Defends Church and Blasts Media," *Caucus, NYT* political blog, http://thecaucus.blogs.nytimes.com/. The parenthetical "normal white folks" is in the original. The spelling and punctuation errors are present in this blog posting and others quoted here.

94. Matt Bai, "Is Obama the End of Black Politics?" *New York Times Magazine,* August 10, 2008, 36–55.

95. Ibid., 37.

96. For the evolution of northern black politics and the role that structural racism and white ethnics played in its development, see the fine article by David Gerber, "A Politics of Limited Options: Northern Black Politics and the Problem of Change and Continuity in Race Relations Historiography," *Journal of Social History* 14, no. 2 (Winter 1980): 235–55. See also Ira Katznelson, *When Affirmative Action Was White* (New York: Norton, 2003). For white reaction to quotas and busing, black militance, and ghetto crime, see Jonathan Rieder, *Canarsie: The Jews and Italians of Brooklyn against Liberalism* (Cambridge: Harvard University Press, 1985).

97. Gore Vidal, *Imperial America: Reflections on the United States of Amnesia* (New York: Nation Books, 2005), 7.

98. Patricia J. Williams, "Let Them Eat Waffles," *Nation,* May 19, 2008, 9.

99. For Afrocentrism, see Asante, *Afrocentricity;* and Molefi Kete

Asante, *An Afrocentric Manifesto: Toward an African Renaissance* (New York: Polity, 2007). Both of these books by Asante are repetitious and not very interesting for the broadly read.

100. See, for example, Asante, *Afrocentricity;* and Molefi K. Asante, *The Afrocentric Idea* (Philadelphia: Temple University Press, 1998).

101. Wright, *What Makes You So Strong?* See also Wright's *Africans Who Shaped Our Faith* (Chicago: Urban Ministries, 1995).

102. Ibid., 20.

103. For Romantic racialism in North America, see Fredrickson, *The Black Image in the White Mind,* 168–70.

104. Hopkins, *Heart and Head,* 18.

105. Obama, *Dreams from My Father,* 198.

106. On this point, see V. Y. Mudimbe, *The Invention of Africa: Gnosis, Philosophy, and the Order of Knowledge* (Bloomington: Indiana University Press, 1988); and V. Y. Mudimbe, *The Idea of Africa* (Bloomington: Indiana University Press, 1994).

107. Quoted in Clarence E. Walker, *Deromanticizing Black History: Critical Essays and Reappraisals* (Knoxville: University of Tennessee Press, 1991), 43.

108. For an excellent discussion of enslavement, the Middle Passage, seasoning, and the arrival of slaves in America, see Ira Berlin, *Many Thousands Gone: The First Two Centuries of Slavery in North America* (Cambridge: Belknap Press of Harvard University Press, 1998); David Eltis, *The Rise of African Slavery in the Americas* (Cambridge: Cambridge University Press, 2000); David Brion Davis, *Inhuman Bondage: The Rise and Fall of Slavery in the New World* (Oxford: Oxford University Press, 2006); and Stephanie Smallwood, *Saltwater Slavery: A Middle Passage from Africa to American Diaspora* (Cambridge: Harvard University Press, 2007).

109. Wright, *What Makes You So Strong?* 136.

110. Ibid., 66.

111. Volkov, *Germans, Jews, and Antisemites,* 202.

112. Mende Nazer, *Slave: My True Story* (New York: Public Affairs, 2003).

113. Wright, *What Makes You So Strong?* 104.

2. "I Don't Want People to Pretend I'm Not Black"

1. Rogak, ed., *In His Own Words*, 134.

2. Barack Obama, "A More Perfect Union," in *Change We Can Believe In: Barack Obama's Plan to Renew America's Promise* (New York: Canongate, 2008), 225–42.

3. Ibid., 225–26. Far from Obama being naively optimistic about America's republican founding, he has recognized the darker side of America's racial history, writing in *The Audacity of Hope* that "the spirit of liberty didn't extend, in the minds of the Founders, to the slaves who worked their fields, made their beds, and nursed their children" (Barack Obama, *The Audacity of Hope: Thoughts on Reclaiming the American Dream* [New York: Three Rivers Press, 2006], 95).

4. "3 Percent of Americans Are Mixed-Race; Census Study Is First of Its Kind," *Washington Times*, April 8, 2005. This figure represented an upward adjustment from the 2.4 percent of Americans who self-identified as "two or more races" in the 2000 Census (see "Who Are We? New Dialogue on Mixed Race," *NYT*, March 31, 2008; see also "Obama Raises Profile of Mixed-Race Americans," *San Francisco Chronicle*, July 21, 2008, http://www.sfgate.com/cgi-bin/article.cgi?f=/c/a/2008/07/20/MNGC11PND8.DTL).

5. U.S. Census Bureau, *Overview of Race and Hispanic Origin: Census 2000 Brief*, March 2001, 3.

6. On the link between "whiteness" and citizenship, see Matthew Frye Jacobson, *Whiteness of a Different Color: European Immigrants and the Alchemy of Race* (Cambridge: Harvard University Press, 1999), 4–5; and Rachel Moran, *Interracial Intimacy: The Regulation of Race and Romance* (Chicago: University of Chicago Press, 2003), 28.

7. Maureen Dowd, "Mud Pies for 'That One,'" *NYT*, October 7, 2008, http://www.nytimes.com/2008/10/08/opinion/08dowd.html?ei=5070&emc=eta1.

8. John Sekora, "Red, White, and Black: Indian Captivities, Colonial Printers, and the Early African-American Narrative," in *A Mixed-Race Ethnicity in Early America*, ed. Frank Shuffelton (New York: Oxford University Press, 1993), 92–104; Gary B. Nash, *Red, White, and Black: The Peoples of Early North America*, 5th ed. (Upper Saddle River, N.J.: Prentice Hall, 2005); Clarence E. Walker, *Mongrel Nation: The America*

Begotten by Thomas Jefferson and Sally Hemings (Charlottesville: University of Virginia Press, 2009); George M. Fredrickson, *White Supremacy: A Comparative Study in American and South African History* (New York: Oxford University Press, 1982), 105.

9. Joel Williamson, *New People: Miscegenation and Mulattoes in the United States* (Baton Rouge: Louisiana State University Press, 1995), 8–11.

10. Andrew Fitzmaurice, "Anticolonialism in Western Political Thought: The Colonial Origins of the Concept of Genocide," in *Empire, Colony, Genocide: Conquest, Occupation, and Subaltern Resistance in World History*, ed. A. Dirk Moses (New York: Berghahn Books, 2008), 67.

11. Joel Williamson, *New People*, 8–11.

12. Ibid., 1.

13. Obama, *Change We Can Believe In*, 225.

14. Ibid., 225–26.

15. Robert Somers, *The Southern States since the War, 1870–1* (Manchester, N.H.: Ayer, 1973), 41.

16. Tali Mendelberg, *The Race Card: Campaign Strategy, Implicit Messages, and the Norm of Equality* (Princeton: Princeton University Press, 2001), 45.

17. Jeff Forret, *Race Relations at the Margins: Slaves and Poor Whites in the Antebellum Southern Countryside* (Baton Rouge: Louisiana State University Press, 2006), 31; James M. O'Toole, *Passing for White: Race, Religion, and the Healy Family, 1820–1920* (Amherst: University of Massachusetts Press, 2003), 70–71.

18. Ariela J. Gross, *What Blood Won't Tell: A History of Race on Trial in America* (Cambridge: Harvard University Press, 2008), 44.

19. David A. Hollinger, *Postethnic America: Beyond Multiculturalism* (New York: Basic Books, 1995), 27; Jerrold M. Packard, *American Nightmare: The History of Jim Crow* (New York: St. Martin's Press, 2002), 98–100; Kerry Rockquemore and David L. Brunsma, *Beyond Black: Biracial Identity in America*, 2nd ed. (Lanham, Md.: Rowan and Littlefield, 2007), 4–5.

20. Antiblack racism, in other words, is historically embedded in the fabric of American culture and the relationships of individuals to different forms of power (see Thomas C. Holt, "Marking: Race, Race-Making, and the Writing of History," *American Historical Review* 100,

no. 1 [February 1995]: 5; Michael Omi and Howard Winant, *Racial Formation in the United States: From the 1960s to the 1990s*, 2nd ed. [New York and London: Routledge, 1994]; Floyd James Davis, *Who Is Black? One Nation's Definition* [University Park: Pennsylvania State University Press, 2001], 4–7; Janis Faye Hutchinson, *Cultural Portrayals of African-Americans: Creating an Ethnic/Racial Identity* [Westport, Conn.: Greenwood, 1997], 52; Elliot Lewis, *Fade: My Journeys in Multiracial America* [New York: Carroll and Graf, 2006], 113; and Werner Sollors, *Interracialism: Black-White Intermarriage in American History, Literature, and Law* [New York: Oxford University Press, 2000], 146–47).

21. Quoted in Joel Williamson, *The Crucible of Race: Black/White/ Relations in the American South since Emancipation* (New York: Oxford University Press, 1984), 41. See also Rachel F. Moran, *Interracial Intimacy: The Regulation of Race and Romance* (Chicago: University of Chicago Press, 2001), 46–48.

22. Lothrop Stoddard, *The Rising Tide of Color against White World Supremacy* (New York: Charles Scribner's Sons, 1922), 12, 19. See, similarly, Josiah Strong, *The New Era or the Coming Kingdom* (New York: Baker and Taylor Co., 1893; and Homer Lea, *The Valor of Ignorance* (New York: Harper and Brothers, 1909), 11.

23. George M. Fredrickson, *The Black Image in the White Mind: The Debate on Afro-American Character and Destiny, 1817–1914* (Middletown: Wesleyan University Press, 1987), 64; James A. Monroe, *Hellfire Nation: The Politics of Sin in American History* (New Haven: Yale University Press, 2004), 177.

24. Lothrop Stoddard, *The Revolt against Civilization: The Menace of the Under Man* (New York: Charles Scribner's Sons, 1924), 88. The related issues of race and sex were also addressed by Alexander Harvey Shannon, *Racial Integrity and Other Features of the Negro Problem* (1907; repr., New York: Books for Libraries Press, 1972), 10, 94. Ulysses G. Weatherly, "Race and Marriage," *American Journal of Sociology* 15, no. 4 (January 1910): 442–43; Frank H. Hankins, *The Racial Basis of Civilization: A Critique of the Nordic Doctrine* (New York: Knopf, 1926), 346; Joseph K. Folsom, "Changing Values in Sex and Family Relations," *American Sociological Review* 2, no. 5 (October 1937): 720; Ray E. Baber, *Marriage and the Family* (New York: McGraw-Hill, 1939); *American Anthropologist* 14, no. 1 (January–March 1912): 156; Milton L. Barron,

People Who Intermarry: Intermarriage in a New England Industrial Community (Syracuse: Syracuse University Press, 1946), 57.

25. Alecia P. Long, *The Great Southern Babylon: Sex, Race, and Respectability in New Orleans, 1865–1920* (Baton Rouge: Louisiana State University Press, 2004), 53–54.

26. Williamson, *Crucible of Race,* 465.

27. Richard Wright, *Native Son* (1940; New York: Perennial, 2001), 67. Similar reflections are contained in James Weldon Johnson, *The Autobiography of an Ex-Coloured Man* (1912; New York: Vintage Books, 1989); Nella Larsen, *"Quicksand" and "Passing,"* ed. Deborah E. McDowell (New Brunswick, N.J.: Rutgers University Press, 2000); and George Schuyler, *Black No More: Being an Account of the Strange and Wonderful Workings of Science in the Land of the Free, A.D. 1933–1940* (1931; College Park, Md.: McGrath, 1969).

28. "Obama's Speech on Race," in Obama, *Change We Can Believe In,* 226–27.

29. Obama, *Dreams from My Father,* 81–82; "Barack Obama's Inaugural Address: Transcript," *NYT,* January 20, 2009, http://www.nytimes.com/2009/01/20/us/politics/20text-obama.html?adxnnl=1&emc=eta1&adxnnlx=1232712151-NzQAS1ZI8HcKvmnR4mmmWA.

30. See, for example, Gail Bederman, *Manliness and Civilization: A Cultural History of Gender and Race in the United States, 1880–1917* (Chicago: University of Chicago Press, 1995), 138; Williamson, *New People,* 115; Kate Millet, *Sexual Politics* (1969; repr., Urbana: University of Illinois Press, 2000), 226; Gail Hawkes, *Sex and Pleasure in Western Culture* (Malden, Mass.: Polity Press, 2004), 129, 150. The sexual fears that accompanied American racial anxieties were evident in the brutal way in which many white communities sought to protect their version of a "more perfect union" by sadistically lynching African American men (see Arthur F. Franklin, *The Tragedy of Lynching* [New York: Dover, 2003], 27–29; Michael J. Pfeifer, *Rough Justice: Lynching and American Society, 1874–1947* (Urbana: University of Illinois Press, 2004), 7–12, passim; and Ken Gonzales-Day, *Lynching in the West, 1850–1935* [Durham: Duke University Press, 2006]).

31. Obama, *Dreams from My Father,* 11.

32. Obama, *Change We Can Believe In,* 227–28, 231.

33. Thomas Dixon, *The Clansman: An Historical Romance of the Ku*

Klux Klan (1905; repr. Alcester, Warwickshire: Read Books, 2008), 294; Williamson, *Crucible of Race*, 152, 158, 162, 165.

34. Dixon, *The Clansman*, 190.

35. Williamson, *Crucible of Race*, 173.

36. Joseph Boskin, *Sambo: The Rise and Demise of an American Jester* (New York: Oxford University Press, 1986), 150; David W. Blight, *Race and Reunion: The Civil War in American Memory* (Cambridge: Harvard University Press, 2001), 81.

37. The National Association for the Advancement of Colored People (NAACP) protested Griffith's film, claiming that it used racist depictions of black people. Griffith responded that he was "a mere filmmaker with no political or ideological view in mind" (see Bonnie M. Anderson, *News Flash: Journalism, Infotainment, and the Bottom-Line Business of Broadcast News* [San Francisco: Jossey-Bass, 2004], 199; Donald Bogle, *Toms, Coons, Mulattoes, Mammies, and Bucks: An Interpretative History of Blacks in American Films* [New York: Continuum, 2001], 16, 10; and Michael P. Rogin, *"Ronald Reagan," the Movie: And Other Episodes in Political Demonology* [Berkeley and Los Angeles: University of California Press, 1987], 207).

38. Bogle, *Toms, Coons, Mulattoes*, 12; Rogin, *"Ronald Reagan," the Movie*, 210.

39. Bogle, Toms, *Coons, Mulattoes*, 13; Rogin, *"Ronald Reagan," the Movie*, 192.

40. In the context of America's uncomfortable history with race mixing, it is worth pondering whether Obama's candidacy would have been as successful if he had been married to a white woman. Moreover, would Obama's life story have the same emotional traction if his mother had been an unemployed black woman and his father white?

41. http://www.city-data.com/forum/elections/372135-obamas-corrupt-past-history.html. The spelling and punctuation errors are present in the blog posting. Similar views were expressed on right-leaning blogs during the 2008 election season (see, for, example http://www.capitolhillblue.com/cont/node/4721; and http://brainshavings.com/2008/10/acorn-obamas-corrupt-community-organizers.html).

42. Edward Reuter, *Race Mixture: Studies in Intermarriage and Miscegenation* (New York: McGraw-Hill, 1931), 126, 187, 198, 213; Eleanor Bodenhorn, "The Mulatto Advantage: The Biological Consequences of

Complexion in Rural Antebellum Virginia," *Journal of Interdisciplinary History* 33, no. 1 (Summer 2002): 21–46.

43. Earnest S. Cox, *Let My People Go* (Richmond, Va.: White American Society, 1925), 7.

44. Quoted on http://www.youtube.com/watch?v=FchvGYkvt3s.

45. Bogle, *Toms, Coons, Mulattoes*, 147–48.

46. Ibid., 147.

47. Gunnar Myrdal, *An American Dilemma: The Negro Problem and American Democracy* (1944; repr., New Brunswick: Transaction, 1996), 1:105.

48. Grove Samuel Dow, *Society and Its Problems: An Introduction to the Principles of Sociology* (1920; New York: Thomas Y. Crowell, 1937), 195.

49. Mike Soraghan, "Westmoreland Calls Obama 'Uppity,'" *The Hill*, http://thehill.com/leading-the-news/westmoreland-calls-obama-uppity-2008-09-04.html.

50. *Philadelphia Inquirer*, November 19, 2004.

51. Charles Barkley, *Who's Afraid of a Large Black Man?* (New York: Riverhead Books, 2006), 17.

52. "'Obama' Monkey Racism Claim," Multimedia section, *Sydney Morning Herald*, October 14, 2008, www.smh.com.au.

53. *Nation*, August 5, 2008, http://www.thenation.com/blogs/notion/342063/print. Country music has a long tradition of identifying with white, blue-collar, right-wing political causes, a tradition that dates back to the 1950s (see Bill C. Malone, *Don't Get Above Your Raisin': Country Music and the Southern Working Class* [Urbana: University of Illinois Press, 2002], 209–11).

54. Obama, *Dreams from My Father*, 11. For "miscegenation," see David G. Croly, *Miscegenation: The Theory of the Blending of the Races Applied to the American White Man and Negro* (New York: H. Dexter, Hamilton, 1864).

55. W. E. B. Du Bois, *The Souls of Black Folk: Essays and Sketches*, 7th ed. (Chicago: A. C. McClurg, 1907), 3.

56. Obama, *Dreams from My Father*, xv.

57. Rogak, ed., *Obama in His Own Words*, 97.

58. During the hotly contested Democratic primary in South Carolina, Robert L. Johnson, the founder of BET, likened Obama to Sidney

Poitier's character in the 1967 movie *Look Who's Coming to Dinner* (see Katherine Q. Seelye, "BET Founder Slams Obama in South Carolina," *NYT,* January 13, 2008, http://thecaucus.blogs.nytimes.com/2008/01/13/bet-chief-raps-obama-in-sc/?ex=1357880400&en=a0b5d830dd91fbca&ei=5088&partner=rssnyt&emc=rss). The British journalist John Pilger used more blunt language, referring to Obama as "a glossy Uncle Tom who would bomb Pakistan" (see John Pilger, "The Danse Macabre of US-Style Democracy," January 23, 2008, http://www.johnpilger.com/page.asp?partid=471).

59. Obama, *Change We Can Believe In,* 227.

60. Shirlee Taylor Haizlip, *The Sweeter the Juice: A Family Memoir in Black and White* (New York: Simon and Schuster, 1994), 15.

61. Edward Ball, *Slaves in the Family* (New York: Ballantine Books, 1998); Essie Mae Washington-Williams, *Dear Senator: A Memoir by the Daughter of Strom Thurmond* (New York: Regan Books, 2005); Rebecca Walker, *Black, White, and Jewish: Autobiography of a Shifting Self* (New York: Riverhead Books, 2001). See also Leslie Alexander Lacy, *The Rise and Fall of a Proper Negro* (New York: Macmillan, 1970), 129; Claudine C. O'Hearn, *Half and Half: Writers on Growing Up Biracial and Bicultural* (New York: Pantheon Books, 1998); June Cross, *Secret Daughter: A Mixed-Race Daughter and the Mother Who Gave Her Away* (New York: Viking, 2006); John A. Martin Jr., *When White Is Black* (Stillwater, Minn.: River's Bend Press, 2005); Bliss Broyard, *One Drop: My Father's Hidden Life—A Story of Race and Family Secrets* (New York: Little, Brown, 2007). The United States is not alone in producing personal stories that reflect the heartache and family drama caused by interracial sex and mixed-race identity. For memoirs from Australia and South Africa, see, for instance, Sally Morgan, *My Place* (Fremantle: Fremantle Arts Centre Press, 1987); Doris Pilkington, *Follow the Rabbit-Proof Fence* (St. Lucia: University of Queensland Press, 1996); and Judith Stone, *When She Was White: The True Story of a Family Divided by Race* (New York: Miramax, 2007).

62. Obama, *Dreams from My Father,* 15.

63. Richard Hofstadter, *Anti-Intellectualism in American Life* (New York: Knopf, 1963), 188; Amber R. Clifford, "Prostitution and Reform in Kansas City, 1880–1930," in *The Other Missouri History: Populists,*

Prostitutes, and Regular Folk, ed. Thomas Morris Spencer (Columbia: University of Missouri Press, 2004), 225–26.

64. Obama, *Dreams from My Father,* 14.

65. Ibid., 18.

66. John Lewis Gillin, Clarence Gus Dittmer, and Roy Jefferson Colbert, *Social Problems* (New York and London: Century, 1928), 229, 449; Charles M. Christian and Sari Bennett, *Black Saga: The African American Experience: A Chronology* (Washington, D.C.: Civitas/Counterpoint, 1999), 192; Dominic J. Capeci, *The Lynching of Cleo Wright* (Lexington: University of Kentucky Press, 1998), 45

67. Bureau of the Census, *Census of the Population: 1960,* vol. 1, *Characteristics of the Population,* pt. 13, "Hawaii" (Washington, D.C.: U.S. Government Printing Office, 1963), xx, 16.

68. Obama, *Dreams from My Father,* 50–51.

69. Ibid., 10.

70. Ibid., 24.

71. Manning Marable, *Race, Reform, and Rebellion: The Second Reconstruction in Black America, 1945–1990* (Jackson: University of Mississippi Press, 1991), 36–38; Douglas S. Massey, "Residential Segregation and Persistent Urban Poverty," in *Civil Rights and Social Wrongs: Black-White Relations since World War II,* ed. John Higham (University Park: Pennsylvania State University Press, 1997), 102–3.

72. John L. Jackson, *Real Black: Adventures in Racial Sincerity* (Chicago: University of Chicago Press, 2005), 277 n. 74; Rogak, ed., *Obama in His Own Words,* 95.

73. Obama, *Dreams from My Father,* 24–25.

74. University of Virginia, Historical Census Browser, http://fisher.lib.virginia.edu/collections/stats/histcensus/php/county.php.

75. Kathryn Waddell Takara, "The African Diaspora in Nineteenth-Century Hawaii," in *They Followed the Trade Winds: African Americans in Hawaii,* ed. Miles M. Jackson (Honolulu: University of Hawaii Press, 2004), 17.

76. Miles M. Jackson, "Prelude to a New Century," in *They Followed the Trade Winds,* ed. Jackson, 55.

77. Quoted in ibid., 58.

78. Theodore Richards, "The Future of the Japanese in Hawaii,"

Journal of Race Development 2 (1911–12): 406, 411; "Hawaii's New Race Product," *American Review of Reviews* (June 1911): 740–41; "Miscegenation in Hawaii," *Journal of Heredity* 8, no. 1 (January 1917): 12; William C. Farabee, *An Anthropometric Study of Hawaiians of Pure and Mixed Blood* (Cambridge: Harvard University Press, 1928).

79. David A. Hollinger, "Amalgamation and Hypodescent: The Question of Ethnoracial Mixture in the History of the United States," *American Historical Review* 108, no. 5 (December 2003): 1364.

80. E. A. Hooton, "Progress in the Study of Race Mixtures with Special Reference to Work Carried on at Harvard University," *Proceedings of the American Philosophical Society* 65 (1926): 319.

81. David E. Stannard, *Honor Killing: How the Infamous "Massie Affair" Transformed Hawaii* (New York: Viking, 2005).

82. Obama, *Dreams from My Father,* 80, 86.

83. Ibid., 73.

84. Robert B. Toplin, "Between Black and White: Attitudes toward Southern Mulattoes, 1830–1861," *Journal of Southern History* 45, no. 2 (May 1979): 194. See also Elmer P. Martin and Joanne M. Martin, *The Black Extended Family* (Chicago: University of Chicago Press, 1980), 96; Williamson, *New People,* 32; John Hope Franklin, *The Free Negro in North Carolina, 1790–1860* (Chapel Hill: University of North Carolina Press, 1995), 36–38; and Deborah Gray White, *Ar'n't I a Woman?: Female Slaves in the Plantation South* (New York: Norton, 1985), 27–61.

85. Willard B. Gatewood, *Aristocrats of Color: The Black Elite, 1880–1920* (Fayetteville: University of Arkansas Press, 2000), 9–10, 160, 163–64, 169; Obiagele Lake, *Blue Veins and Kinky Hair: Naming and Color Consciousness in African America* (Westport, Conn: Praeger, 2003), 2; Smithers, *Science, Sexuality, and Race,* 160–62.

86. Kathy Russell, *The Color Complex* (New York: Anchor Books, 1993), 27; Ayana D. Boyd and Lori L. Tharps, *Hair Story: Untangling the Roots of Black Hair in America* (New York: St. Martin's Press, 2001), 22.

87. Peter J. Boyer, "The Color of Politics: A Mayor in the Post-Racial Generation," *New Yorker,* February 4, 2008, 40; "Jackson Apologizes for 'Crude' Obama Remarks," CNN, July 9, 2008, http://www.cnn.com/2008/POLITICS/07/09/jesse.jackson.comment/.

88. Obama, *Dreams from My Father,* 211.

89. Andrew Delbanco, "Deconstructing Barry: A Literary Critic Reads Obama," *New Republic*, July 9, 2008, 20.

90. John B. Judas, "The Big Race: Obama and the Psychology of the Color Barrier," *New Republic*, May 28, 2008, 21–24.

91. "Remarks of Senator Barack Obama: The America We Love," *Washington Post*, June 30, 2008, http://voices.washingtonpost.com/44/2008/06/30/obamas_patriotism_speech.html.

92. Darryl Fears, "Black Community Is Increasingly Protective of Obama," *Washington Post*, May 10, 2008.

93. "Election Results 2008—Exit Polls," *NYT*, http://elections.nytimes.com/2008/results/president/map.html?scp=1&sq=election%20results,%202008&st=cse.

94. Stephen Middleton, *Black Congressmen during Reconstruction: A Documentary Sourcebook* (Westport, Conn.: Greenwood Press, 2002).

95. Howard N. Rabinowitz, "Three Reconstruction Leaders: Blanche K. Bruce, Robert Brown Elliot, and Holland Thompson," in *Black Leaders of the Nineteenth Century*, ed. Leon Litwack and August Meier (Urbana: University of Illinois Press, 1991), 192.

96. Stanley Turkel, *Heroes of the American Reconstruction: Profiles of Sixteen Educators, Politicians and Activists* (Jefferson, N.C.: McFarland, 2005), 128.

97. A transcript of Giuliani's speech is available at the *New York Times*, http://elections.nytimes.com/2008/president/conventions/videos/20080903_GIULIANI_SPEECH.html?scp=1&sq=giuliani%20rnc%20speech&st=cse.

98. Dwight N. Hopkins and George C. L. Cummings, eds., *Cut Loose Your Stammering Tongue: Black Theology in the Slave Narratives* (Louisville: Westminster John Knox Press, 2003), 7.

99. Leon F. Litwack, *Trouble in Mind: Black Southerners in the Age of Jim Crow* (New York: Vintage Books, 1999), 285; Gatewood, *Aristocrats of Color*, 7.

100. Thomas Holt, *Black over White: Negro Political Leadership in South Carolina during Reconstruction* (Urbana: University of Illinois Press, 1977), 12.

101. Benjamin Quarles, *Black Abolitionists* (New York: Oxford University Press, 1969); Hanes Walton Jr., *Invisible Politics: Black Political*

Behavior (Albany: SUNY Press, 1985), 91–92; Richard S. Newman, *The Transformation of American Abolitionism: Fighting Slavery in the Early Republic* (Chapel Hill: University of North Carolina Press, 2001); Patrick Rael, *Black Identity and Black Protest in the Antebellum North* (Chapel Hill: University of North Carolina Press, 2002).

102. John Hope Franklin, *Reconstruction after the Civil War* (Chicago: University of Chicago Press, 1961), 93

103. Holt, *Black over White*, 27.

104. Obama, *Change We Can Believe In*, 226.

105. Elliot M. Rudwick, "Oscar De Priest and the Jim Crow Restaurant in the U.S. House of Representatives," *Journal of Negro Education* 35, no. 1 (Winter 1966): 77; David S. Day, "Herbert Hoover and Racial Politics: The De Priest Incident," *Journal of Negro History* 65, no. 1 (Winter 1980): 6–17.

106. Julie Winch, *The Elite of Our People: Sketches of Black Upper-Class Life in Antebellum Philadelphia* (University Park: Pennsylvania State University Press, 2000), 73; Michele Mitchell, *Righteous Propagation: African Americans and the Politics of Racial Destiny after Reconstruction* (Chapel Hill: University of North Carolina Press, 2004), 62, passim.

107. David G. Croly, *Miscegenation: The Theory of the Blending of the Races Applied to the American White Man and Negro* (New York: H. Dexter, Hamilton, 1864); James Hugo Johnson, *Miscegenation in the Antebellum South* (New York: AMS Press, 1972); Williamson, *New People*; Smithers, *Science, Sexuality, and Race*, chap. 2.

108. *NYT*, February 2, 1875.

109. *San Francisco Bulletin*, March 22, 1862.

110. Franklin, *Reconstruction*, 65.

111. Jason Deparle, "Republicans Receive an Obama Parody to Mixed Reviews," *NYT*, December 28, 2008, http://query.nytimes.com/gst/fullpage.html?res=9C07E2DA133DF93BA15751C1A96E9C8B63&scp=5&sq=barack%20the%20magic%20negro&st=cse.

112. Obama, *Change We Can Believe In*, 235–36.

113. Ibid., 237–38.

114. Eric L. McKitrick, *Andrew Johnson and Reconstruction* (New York: Oxford University Press, 1988), 38.

115. Bertram W. Doyle, *The Etiquette of Race Relations* (Chicago: University of Chicago Press, 1937); Oliver C. Cox, *Caste, Class, and Race:*

A Study of Social Dynamics (New York: Monthly Review Press, 1959), 14–24; Jennifer L. Ritterhouse, *Growing Up Jim Crow: How Black and White Southern Children Learned Race* (New York: Rowan and Littlefield, 2006), 24–26; *The Liberator*, August 22, 1862, in *Black Workers: A Documentary History from Colonial Times to the Present*, ed. Philip S. Foner and Ronald L. Lewis (Philadelphia: Temple University Press, 1989), 123 (italics in original).

116. Quoted in *Black Workers*, ed. Foner and Lewis, 124.

117. C. Van Woodward, *Origins of the New South, 1877–1913* (1951; Baton Rouge: Louisiana State University Press, 1971), 222.

118. Eric Foner, *Reconstruction: America's Unfinished Revolution, 1863–1877* (New York: Harper and Row, 1988), 133.

119. *American Federationist* (April 1901), in *Black Workers*, ed. Foner and Lewis, 243. In a comment typical of white working-class hostility to black workers, the union activist and Populist political leader Tom Watson complained that the stymieing of a populist political movement in the South "may be boiled down to one word—nigger" (see C. Van Woodward, *Tom Watson: Agrarian Rebel* [New York: Oxford University Press, 1963], 370; see also Charles Crowe, "Tom Watson, Populist and Blacks Reconsidered," *Journal of Negro History* 55, no. 2 [April 1970], 104; and Nick Salvatore, *Eugene V. Debs: Citizen and Socialist* [Urbana: University of Illinois Press, 1982], 226–28, 105).

120. Marc Ambinder, "Race Over?" *Atlantic*, January–February 2009, http://www.theatlantic.com/doc/200901/obama-race.

121. Roy Wilkins, *Standing Fast: The Autobiography of Roy Wilkins*, with Tom Mathews (New York: Da Capo Press, 1994), 292. See also Harvard Sitkoff, "Racial Militancy and Interracial Violence in the Second World War," *Journal of American History* 58, no. 3 (December 1971): 662; and Lee Finkle, "The Conservative Aims of Militant Rhetoric: Black Protest during World War II," *Journal of American History* 60, no. 3 (December 1973): 692–713.

122. Robert E. Weems, *Desegregating the Dollar: African American Consumerism in the Twentieth Century* (New York: New York University Press, 1998), 60; Charles M. Payne, *I've Got the Light of Freedom: The Organizing Tradition and the Mississippi Freedom Struggle* (Berkeley and Los Angeles: University of California Press, 1996), 118, 129–30, 250, 256, 275; Glenn T. Eskew, *But for Birmingham: The Local and National*

Movements in the Civil Rights Struggle (Chapel Hill: University of North Carolina Press, 1997), 14–16, 53, 59; Andrew M. Manis, *A Fire You Can't Put Out: The Civil Rights Life of Birmingham's Reverend Fred Shuttlesworth* (Tuscaloosa: University of Alabama Press, 1999), 2, 48, 55, 58–59, 118, 121.

123. Obama, *The Audacity of Hope*, 29.

124. Ibid., 242–43.

125. Martin Luther King Jr., *Why We Can't Wait* (1963; repr., New York: Signet Classics, 2000), 9. King's emphasis on the economics of American racism were, and continue to be, overlooked in preference for his more optimistic statements about racial harmony. For example, King said of the uneven nature of American racial "progress" that "we have advanced in some areas from all-out unrestrained resistance to a sophisticated form of delay embodied in tokenism." In some areas of American social and economic life, King's words remain as trenchant in the twenty-first century as they were in the 1960s (James M. Washington, ed., *A Testament of Hope: The Essential Writings of Martin Luther King, Jr.* [San Francisco: Harper and Row, 1986], 100; see also Clayborne Carson, ed., *The Papers of Martin Luther King, Jr.*, vol. 4, *The Symbol of the Movement, January 1957–December 1958* [Berkeley and Los Angeles: University of California Press, 1992], 435; and Mary L. Dudziak, *Cold War Civil Rights: Race and the Image of American Democracy* [Princeton: Princeton University Press, 2000]).

126. Obama, *The Audacity of Hope*, 253–54.

127. Bayard Rustin, "'Black Power' and Coalition Politics," *Commentary* 42, no. 3 (September 1966): 38. See also John White, *Black Leadership in America, 1895–1968* (New York: Longman, 1985), 101; Essien-Udom, *Black Nationalism*, 4; C. Eric Lincoln, *The Black Muslims in America* (Boston: Beacon Press, 1973), 4, 8; Milton D. Morris, *The Politics of Black America* (New York: Harper and Row, 1975), 91; William L. Van Deburg, *New Day in Babylon: The Black Power Movement and American Culture, 1965–1975* (Chicago: University of Chicago Press, 1992), chap. 5; William L. Van Deburg, *Modern Black Nationalism: From Marcus Garvey to Louis Farrakhan* (New York: New York University Press, 1997), 85–94, 136–43, 275.

128. Obama, *Dreams from My Father*, 202–3.

129. Stephen Steinberg, *The Ethnic Myth: Race, Ethnicity, and Class in America* (Boston: Beacon Press, 2001), 251–52; Paul Kivel, *Uprooting Racism: How White People Can Work for Racial Justice* (Gabriola Island, B.C.: New Society, 2002), 61, 68, 90; Steve Martinot, *The Rule of Racialization: Class, Identity, Governance* (Philadelphia: Temple University Press, 2003), 140–42.

130. Rick Perlstein, *Nixonland: The Rise of a President and the Fracturing of America* (New York: Scribner, 2008), 279.

131. *U.S. News & World Report*, cited in Richard Lentz, *Symbols, the News Magazines, and Martin Luther King* (Baton Rouge: Louisiana State University Press, 1990), 175. See also Adam Fairclough, *To Redeem the Soul of America*, 172–73; and Stephen B. Oates, *Let the Trumpet Sound: The Life of Martin Luther King, Jr.* (New York: New American Library, 1982), 299.

132. Perlstein, *Nixonland*, 119.

133. Roger Hewitt, *White Backlash and the Politics of Multiculturalism* (Cambridge: Cambridge University Press, 2005), 9; Allan J. Lichtman, *White Protestant Nation: The Rise of the American Conservative Movement* (New York: Atlantic Monthly Press, 2008), 130; T. D. Allman, *Rogue State: America at War with the World* (New York: Nation Books, 2004), 209.

134. Hazel Rose Markus, Claude M. Steele, and Dorothy M. Steele, "Colorblindness as a Barrier to Inclusion: Assimilation and Nonimmigrant Minorities," *Daedalus* 129, no. 4 (2000): 234; J. Morgan Kousser, *Colorblind Justice: Minority Voting Rights and the Undoing of the Second Reconstruction* (Chapel Hill: University of North Carolina Press, 1999), 6, 10.

135. Peter N. Carroll, *It Seemed Like Nothing Happened: America in the 1970s* (New Brunswick, N.J.: Rutgers University Press, 1990), xv, 6, 178–79; Alex Mintz, *The Political Economy of Military Spending in the United States* (New York: Routledge, 1992), 270; Alan Wolfe, *One Nation, After All: What Middle-Class Americans Really Think About God, Country, Family, Racism, Welfare, Immigration, Homosexuality, Work, the Right, the Left, and Each Other* (New York: Penguin Books, 1999); John Kane, *The Politics of Moral Capital* (New York: Cambridge University Press, 2001), 23; Kiron K. Skinner, Annelise Anderson, and Martin

Anderson, eds., *Reagan, In His Own Hand* (New York: Free Press, 2001), 385; Jeremy D. Mayer, *Running on Race: Racial Politics in Presidential Campaigns, 1960–2000* (New York: Random House, 2002), chaps. 8 and 9; Juan Williams, *Eyes on the Prize: America's Civil Rights Years, 1954–1965* (New York: Penguin Books, 2002), 38; Linda Burnham, *Racism in U.S. Welfare Policy: A Human Rights Issue* (Oakland, Calif.: Women of Color Resource Center, 2002); Robert Mason, *Richard Nixon and the Quest for a New Majority* (Chapel Hill: University of North Carolina Press, 2004), 63; Charles J. Ogletree, *All Deliberate Speed: Reflections on the First Half-Century of Brown v. Board of Education* (New York: Norton, 2005); Adrian R. Lewis, *The American Culture of War: The History of U.S. Military Force from World War II to Operation Iraqi Freedom* (Boca Raton, Fla.: CRC Press, 2007), 448; Jeremy D. Mayer, "Reagan and Race: Prophet of Colorblindness, Baiter of the Backlash," in *Deconstructing Reagan: Conservative Mythology and America's Fortieth President*, ed. Kyle Longley, Jeremy D. Mayer, Michael Schaller, and John W. Sloan (Armonk, N.Y.: M. E. Sharpe, 2007), 85; Perlstein, *Nixonland*, 277, 285, 300, 598–99.

136. Thomas B. Edsall and Mary D. Edsall, *Chain Reaction: The Impact of Race, Rights, and Taxes on American Politics* (New York: Norton, 1992), 7, 10–12, 41–42, 62; Raymond Wolters, *Right Turn: William Bradford Reynolds, the Reagan Administration, and Black Civil Rights* (New Brunswick, N.J.: Transaction, 1996), 192–93; John Fobanjong, *Understanding the Backlash against Affirmative Action* (Huntington, N.Y.: Nova Science Publishers, 2001), 6–7; Antoine Joseph, "Racial Conflict in the 21st Century: The Formation of a Stable Majority and the African American Predicament," in *The New Black: Alternative Strategies and Paradigms for the 21st Century*, ed. Rodney Coates and Rutledge Dennis (Bingley, U.K.: Emerald Group, 2007), 86; Jeremy D. Mayer, "Reagan and Race: Prophet of Colorblindness, Baiter of the Backlash," in *Deconstructing Reagan*, ed. Longley, Mayer, Schaller, and Sloan, 85.

137. Mayer, *Running on Race*, 6, 97. Adolph Reed Jr. has argued that Republican strategists recognized how "civil-rights laws, and affirmative action in particular, just stir up white hostility, since they are coercive, and an affront to properly market-based notions of justice and equity" (Adolph Reed Jr., "Yackety-Yak about Race," in *Race and Ethnicity in the United States: Issues and Debates*, ed. Stephen Steinberg [Boston: Blackwell, 2000], 61).

138. Obama, *The Audacity of Hope,* 233. On the limits of "color blindness" and "postracialism," see Kousser, *Colorblind Injustice,* 270; and Lewis R. Gordon, *Her Majesty's Other Children: Sketches of Racism from a Neocolonial Age* (Lanham, Md.: Rowman and Littlefield, 1997), 55–56.

139. Obama, *Dreams from My Father,* 274, 278–79.

140. Ibid., 294; see also 280–84.

141. Recalling his college years, Obama offered this scathing indictment of mixed-race identity embodying the ideal "postracial" American. Remembering a conversation he had with a "*multiracial*" woman named Joyce, Obama wrote of how she rejected any suggestion that she was black: "That was the problem with people like Joyce. They talked about the richness of their multicultural heritage and it sounded real good, until you noticed that they avoided black people" (Obama, *Dreams from My Father,* 99). See also the *Boondocks* character Jazmine Dubois, who "is a young biracial girl who struggles to find her identity at the border of the color line" (http://www.amuniversal.com/ups/features/boondocks/chars.htm). For further analysis of the implications of "postrace" ideologies, see Suki Ali, *Mixed-Race, Post-Race: Gender, New Ethnicities and Cultural Practices* (Oxford: Berg, 2003), 2, 9; and C. Richard King, *Native Athletes in Sport and Society: A Reader* (Lincoln: University of Nebraska Press, 2005), 224.

142. Obama, *The Audacity of Hope,* 232. Perhaps reflecting the post–civil rights era in which he writes, Obama observes that America's "familiarity with the lives of the black poor has bred spasms of fear and outright contempt. But mostly it's bred indifference" (253).

143. Ibid., 243.

144. Marcus Marby, "Color Test: Where Whites Draw the Line," *NYT,* June 8, 2008, http://www.nytimes.com/2008/06/08/weekinreview/08mabry.html.

145. Ryan Lizza, "Making It: How Chicago Shaped Obama," *New Yorker,* July 21, 2008, 49–65; Martin Fletcher, "Before He Was Famous: The Truth behind Obama's Meteoric Ascent," *Times* (London), October 14, 2008.

146. Yvonne Bynoe, *Stand and Deliver: Political Activism, Leadership, and Hip Hop Culture* (Brooklyn: Soft Skull Press, 2004), 91; Kevin Mumford, *Newark: A History of Race, Rights, and Riots in America* (New York: New York University Press, 2007), 218–19. For analysis of the

relationship between Booker T. Washington and President Theodore Roosevelt, see Louis R. Harlan, *Booker T. Washington: The Wizard of Tuskegee, 1901–1915* (New York: Oxford University Press, 1986), chap. 1. For a sampling of African American critiques of Obama, see Adolph Reed Jr., "Where Obamaism Seems to Be Going," *Black Agenda Report*, July 16, 2008, http://www.blackagendareport.com; Tyrone Simpson, "Barack Obama and the Abuse of Black Fathers," *Black Agenda Report*, July 23, 2008, http://www.blackagendareport.com.

147. Obama, *Change We Can Believe In*, 232.

148. "Senator Obama's Remarks in N.C.," *NYT*, May 6, 2008.

149. Obama, *Change We Can Believe In*, 235.

150. Ta-Nehisi Coates, "'This Is How We Lost to the White Man': The Audacity of Bill Cosby's Black Conservatism," *Atlantic*, May 2008, 54.

151. Kate Phillips, "Wright Defends Church and Blasts Media," *Caucus, NYT* political blog, April 28, 2008, http://thecaucus.blogs.nytimes.com/2008/04/28/rev-wright-defends-church-blasts-media/?scp=1&sq=%22Wright%20Defends%20Church%20and%20Blasts%20Media%22%20&st=cse. The spelling and punctuation errors are present in the blog posting.

152. See, for example, the blogger who claimed: "Rev. Wright is doing his former associate no favor by going out on press tours at this time. Obama knew he could never win the presidency as the 'race candidate' and did his best to stay away from it until the videos of excerpts of his pastor's sermons hit the internet. Having made a speech about the subject that could not put the entire matter to rest, he has lately been trying to woo the working class voters that he previously alienated" (see Phillips, "Wright Defends Church and Blasts Media," *Caucus, NYT* political blog, April 28, 2008).

153. Michael Cooper, "Comments Bring Wives into the Fray in Wisconsin," *NYT*, February 20, 2008.

154. Ewen MacAskill, "Obama Campaign Finds Prejudice Lingers in Blue-Collar Heartlands," *Guardian* (Manchester), October 14, 2008.

155. Tim Reid, "He Looks Like a Terrorist But I'll Vote for Him Anyway," *Times* (London), October 16, 2008.

156. Ana Maria Alonso, "The Politics of Space, Time and Substance: State Formation, Nationalism and Ethnicity," *Annual Review of Anthro-*

pology 23 (1994): 379–405; Qiong Li and Marilynn B. Brewer, “What Does It Mean to Be an American?: Patriotism, and American Identity after 9/11,” *Political Psychology* 25, no. 5 (October 2004): 727–39.

157. John Solomos and Les Back, *Racism and Society* (Houndsmills, Basingstoke: Macmillan, 1996), 18–19; Ann Laura Stoler, “Racial Histories and Their Regimes of Truth,” in *Political Power and Social Theory,* ed. Diane E. Davis (Greenwich, Conn.: JAI Press, 1997), 183–206; George M. Fredrickson, *Racism: A Short History* (Princeton: Princeton University Press, 2002), 8; Smithers, *Science, Sexuality, and Race,* 5.

158. Obama, *The Audacity of Hope,* 92.

159. Patricia J. Williams, *Seeing a Color-Blind Future: The Paradox of Race* (New York: Noonday Press, 1997), 17.

Epilogue

1. John F. Burns, “Obama Promises the World a Renewed America,” *NYT,* January 20, 2009, http://www.nytimes.com/2009/01/21/us/politics/21abroad.html?scp=7&sq=americans%20united%20for%20inauguration&st=cse; Waleed Aly, “Co-Operation Can Be a Powerful Tool,” *Age,* January 24, 2009, http://www.theage.com.au/opinion/cooperation-can-be-a-powerful-tool-20090123-7onk.html.

2. See, for example, “Inauguration Marks Generational, Racial Turning Point,” *PBS NewsHour,* http://www.pbs.org/newshour/bb/white_house/jan-june09/mlkday_01-19.html; “Three Generations: Little Rock to Obama,” BBC News, http://news.bbc.co.uk/2/hi/in_depth/7831637.stm.

3. “Barack Obama’s Inaugural Address: Transcript,” *NYT,* January 20, 2009.

4. Lucas E. Morel, *Lincoln’s Sacred Effort: Defining Religion’s Role in American Self-Government* (Lanham, Md.: Lexington Books, 2000), 65.

5. Anne Davies, “Obama Retraces Lincoln’s Journey,” *Sydney Morning Herald,* January 19, 2009, http://www.smh.com.au/news/world/anne-davies/2009/01/18/1232213448841.html; Anthony Painter, *Barack Obama: The Movement for Change* (London: BlackAmber Inspirations, 2008), 162–64.

6. “Barack Obama’s Inaugural Address: Transcript,” *NYT,* January 20, 2009.

7. *NYT*, October 10, 2008, http://elections.nytimes.com/2008/results/president/exit-polls.html.

8. Judith Warner, "Tears to Remember," *NYT*, November 6, 2008, http://warner.blogs.nytimes.com/2008/11/06/title/?scp=13&sq=judith%20warner%20+%20obama&st=cse.

9. Michael K. Brown, Martin Carnoy, Elliott Currie, and Troy Duster, *Whitewashing Race: The Myth of a Color-Blind Society* (Berkeley and Los Angeles: University of California Press, 2003), 2.

10. Larry Rohter, "The Klan Chimes in on Obama," *NYT*, November 6, 2008, http://thecaucus.blogs.nytimes.com/2008/11/06/the-klan-chimes-in-on-obama/. Jared Sexton writes of the "realm of the unspeakable," a reference to the difficulty that Americans continue to experience when discussing race, sex, and identity. In 2008, the "realm of the unspeakable" became part of America's political debate (Jared Sexton, *Amalgamation Schemes: Antiblackness and the Critique of Multiculturalism* [Minneapolis: University of Minnesota Press, 2008], 161).

Index